EDUCATION AND TRAINING IN THE EUROPEAN UNION

Education and Training in the European Union

ANDREAS MOSCHONAS
Assistant Professor
Department of Sociology
University of Crete

Ashgate

Aldershot • Brookfield USA • Singapore • Sydney

Published by
Ashgate Publishing Limited
Gower House
Croft Road
Aldershot
Hants GU11 3HR
England

Ashgate Publishing Company
Old Post Road
Brookfield
Vermont 05036
USA

British Library Cataloguing in Publication Data
Moschonas, Andreas
    Education and training in the European Union
    1.Vocational education - European Union countries
    I.Title
    370.1'13'094

Library of Congress Cataloging-in-Publication Data
Moschonas, Andreas.
    Education and training in the European Union / Andreas Moschonas.
        p.   cm.
    Includes bibliographical references and index.
    ISBN 1-84014-067-4 (hc)
    1. Education–European Union countries. 2. Vocational education-
-European Union countries. 3. Education–Social aspects–European
Union countries. 4. Education and state–European Union countries.
5. Education–European Union countries–Finance. I. Title.
LA622.M67   1997
370'.94–dc21   97-41409
                                                                CIP

ISBN 1 84014 067 4

Printed and bound by Athenaeum Press Ltd.,
Gateshead, Tyne & Wear.

Contents

List of Exhibits and Figures

Exhibits

Figures

Preface

The political sociology of European integration has for many years been the main subject of my teaching and research activities. I have mainly been interested in studying the logic of European integration, the building of supranational institutions and the formation of Community policies within a specific historical conjuncture, i.e. one ultimately defined by the prevailing relationship between social-class interests and political power at the sub-national, national and/or Community level.

The social dimension of European integration, aimed at the establishment of a 'social Europe' in a genuine political Community, has been a 'test case' in my EU studies, for it gives by itself a clear indication of the degree and the content of European integration. The study of institutions, processes and policies can become a fruitful exercise only if one tries through it to shed some light on the very classical question 'who gets, what, when, how and why'. Thus the function of redistributing wealth, in association with that of defining values, becomes a key criterion for determining the social content of political power.

The present work on education and vocational training in the Community has been pursued with these very thoughts in mind. It is a modest effort to examine why the EC decided to take action in the fields of education and training, what the extent of this involvement is, and how the future may affect EC decisions on education and training. The clue one gets from the present work is that we should watch more carefully how the relationship between economic integration and political unification unfolds in the years to come.

The bulk of this work was researched and written at the University of Reading, from October 1996 to June 1997, during my sabbatical leave from the University of Crete. I would like to thank Professor Christoph Bluth, Director of the Graduate School of European and International Studies, and Dr Stelios Stavridis, Director of the Centre for Euro-Mediterranean Studies, at the University of Reading, for their assistance during my work and for giving me the opportunity to work in a quiet and intellectually stimulating environment. I also thank Professor Keith Watson, Director of the Centre for International Studies in Education, Management and Training, at the University of Reading, for inviting me to present the conclusions of this work at a Departmental Seminar and thus giving me the opportunity to benefit from the discussion. The staff in the European Documentation Centre in the main Library at the University of Reading were very helpful to me and I am indeed grateful to them. A word of appreciation to Joan Batchelor who kindly read the whole manuscript and made useful comments on grammar and style.

I would also like to thank my colleagues in the Department of Sociology at the University of Crete, and especially Professor Yannis Pirgiotakis, Head of the Department at that time and currently Vice-Rector of the University, who allowed me to take a full-year leave of absence in order to concentrate on my research. Special thanks are due to Dionysis Gravaris who read the whole manuscript and made constructive comments.

Andreas Moschonas
Reading, June 1997

1 Prologue

The social dimension of the European Union (EU[1]) has been an integral part of European integration. It represents a natural complement to the completion of the internal market, due to the fact that the creation of a vast economic area, which is based on the market and business cooperation, requires the establishment of a European social area as well. In Delors's words, the "European social dimension is what allows competition to flourish between undertakings and individuals on a reasonable and fair basis", and thus any attempt "to give new depth to the Common Market which neglected this social dimension would be doomed to failure" (Delors, 1985 quoted in Hantrais, 1995: 6).

As such, the social dimension encompasses areas of social policy competence where initiatives are taken and uniform or at least minimum standards are set at the EU level. These include measures directly related to employment and working conditions, particularly the health, safety, and vocational training of workers as well as the mobility of young people within the Community. The EC education and training programmes were introduced to serve certain of these very objectives, that is, to enable young people to experience the 'reality of Europe' through various forms of cooperation, including training periods in firms in other member states, university courses in other Community countries, and exchanges. All these transnational mobility schemes are thought to represent a vital element of the Community's investment in human resources, by fostering improvement of the understanding of other European societies and cultures, encouraging cooperation between education and research institutions and the world of work, thereby helping to improve the quality of education, training and research, and also by paving the way for the creation of an employment and work area on a Community-wide scale [cf. COM(96)462 final].

In this broad context, the aim of this work is to examine a specific component of the European social dimension, namely the Community's initiatives and actions on education and vocational training. This raises the question: Why has the Community entered the field of education and training? It did so, a Community document states, in order to "encourage commitment to the Community's aims among the younger generations", and also to "promote mobility of human resources, which is a

1

prerequisite for a genuine frontier-free area"[2]. This implies that the Community's actions on education and training have a dual objective, namely to contribute to (i) the completion of the internal market, and (ii) the formation of a Community cultural identity.

The completion of the internal market is associated with the full operation of the four basic economic freedoms which define economic integration. These are the free movement of goods, of capital, of services, and of persons. The latter embraces the free movement of labour as a precondition for the development of a European labour market. In this context education becomes a policy aiming at the improvement of the qualities of human capital, thereby contributing to the enhancement of both the productivity of labour and the competitiveness of the economy. I call this the **social-economic** dimension of education wherein the justification of any interest in educational rights is a consequence of the need to ensure the free movement of labour as an important component in factor mobility.

The formation on the other hand of a European cultural identity is associated with the full operation of the basic political rights and freedoms which define political integration. These are the traditional civil rights and freedoms of equality, justice, expression, association, as well as the political rights of participation in the social and political process, as a precondition for the development of a European political community. In this context education becomes a policy directed towards the improvement of the qualities of the self and of the community, as individuals and as citizens. This, thereby, contributes to the enhancement of both the individual satisfaction and the political effectiveness or stability. I call this the **cultural-political** dimension of education wherein educational rights are associated with citizenship rights, i.e. with the need to strengthen the protection of the rights and interests of the nationals of the member states, through the introduction of a citizenship of the Union[3].

The social-economic dimension of education is a function of economic integration, whereas the cultural-political dimension of education becomes a function of political integration. This means that the advancement of the process of economic integration necessitates EU measures on education designed to respond to the demands and to improve the qualities of the labour market. While the advancement of the process of political integration makes imperative the adoption of EU measures on education with the aim of improving the conditions for political legitimisation (see chapter 2).

There are two main channels through which the Community can advance its presence in the field of education and training. One is **institutional** which entails the adoption of overriding policy principles expressed in constitutional, legislative or even executive terms. The other, which derives from the first, is **financial** and refers to the Community's influence in education and training as a result of the 'power of the purse' via the various funding programmes[4]. In the institutional area the Community has progressively established a broad framework within which specific measures have been introduced in relation to various education topics such as information on education and training, mobility and cooperation between education institutions, as well as initial, continuing and advanced training. The key characteristics of these measures are, firstly, the low degree of Community enforcement and, secondly, the dominance of a utilitarian principle which gives primacy to vocational training as opposed to education proper (see chapter 3).

In the financial area the Community has indeed increased the magnitude of funding through both the Social Fund and the various education and training programmes. These programmes were mainly introduced in the last fifteen years in an effort to advance education and training objectives in key areas, such as the learning of foreign languages, initial education and training, inter-university cooperation between member states, and cooperation between higher education institutions and industry. The key characteristic of these operations, however, is the low degree of Community financial involvement in education and training, and thus the inability of the Community to transform its piecemeal actions into a coherent education and training policy (see chapter 4).

The gap between maximalist declarations and minimalist actions, itself derived from the existing discrepancy between advanced economic integration and loose political construction, leaves education and training in the Community with endemic deficiencies and contradictions. These mainly unfold in the contrasting areas of harmonisation vs cooperation and academic vs professional, with particular reference to the recognition of diplomas, the relationship between education proper and vocational training, and the role of the university in the context of higher education (see chapter 5).

The underlying argument in this work is that an appreciation of the magnitude of these deficiencies and contradictions requires a better understanding of the relationship between state and education, both in the member states and in the process of European integration. The role of the political authorities in relation to education and training cannot be confined only to the requirements of the economy and the reproduction of human capital, for it also includes the political imperatives of socialisation and legitimisation. Thus viewed, the education and training actions of the Community cannot but represent an unstable compromise conditioned by the political conjuncture. In this context I argue (chapter 6) that the pace of **political** integration ultimately conditions the Community's competence in the field of education.

Notes

1 Unless otherwise indicated, throughout this work the terms European Community (EC) and European Union (EU) will be used interchangeably.
2 From the 1986 Commission programme, published in Bulletin of the European Communities, Supplement 1/86, p.21.
3 The concept of 'citizenship' was introduced only with the EU Treaty, while prior to that the EC knew only 'workers' and thus its interest in education and training had a 'market-related' justification (cf. Hantrais, 1995: 197–99).
4 These channels have historically been employed by all governments in federal political systems where responsibility over education usually remains with local authorities (cf. Lonbay, 1989: 364).

2 The Analytical Framework

The two dimensions of education introduced above, i.e. the 'socio-economic' and the 'cultural-political', derive from well-established theoretical paradigms. Specifically, the former can theoretically be expressed within the analytical framework of the so-called 'human capital' approach, in which education and training expenditures represent investment in human capital, while the latter is informed by both the theoretical statements on 'liberal education' and the critical theories on the ideological role of education.

2.1 The Human Capital Approach

The birth of the human capital approach is said to be on the 28th of December 1960, at the seventy-third annual meeting of the American Economic Association, where the then President of the Association, Theodore Schultz, delivered his Presidential Address on 'investment in human capital' (Schultz, 1961; Blaug, 1992). The argument put forward by Schultz was that skills and knowledge are a form of capital, called human capital. The analysts who subsequently worked on the basis of this assumption not only looked upon education from a utilitarian point of view, but also proposed theoretical statements characterised by 'methodological individualism' according to which all social phenomena must be traced back to their foundation in individual behaviour. In this sense the human capital analysts became true descendants of the classical and neo-classical economic theorists (Blaug, 1992; West, 1992).

In fact, theorists such as A. Smith, J.S. Mill and A. Marshall, for instance, highlighted the importance of education as a form of investment. For A. Smith, who views rational self-interest as the foundation of human action and association, the division of labour contributes to the productive powers of labour by increasing the 'dexterity' of the workers. The workers, however, have to acquire entrepreneurial and other skills through education and training. The common people, A. Smith argues, who spend their lives in varied occupations, chiefly manual, and whose parents cannot look after their interests, need the attention of the public, in a civilised and commercial society. This means that the state should facilitate, encourage, and even "impose upon almost the whole body of the people, the necessity of acquiring those most essential parts of education", namely "reading, writing, and arithmetic", before "they can be employed in those occupations" (A. Smith, 1961 [1776]: 304–305. cf. Vaizey, 1962: 15–16; Bray, 1990: 253–54).

In a similar socio-historical conjuncture, J.S. Mill perceives labour as an agent of production and calls for actions aimed to alter the 'habits' of the labouring people. These include (i) an "effective national education of the children of the labouring class", and (ii) a system of measures suitable to "extinguish extreme poverty for one whole generation" (J.S. Mill, 1878: 465). Thus, like A. Smith, J.S. Mill sees education as one of those things in which "it is admissible in principle that a government should provide for the people". For, J.S. Mill argues, education "cannot be paid for, at its full cost, from the common wages of unskilled labour", and that when there are certain basic elements of knowledge which "all human beings born into the community should acquire during childhood" (J.S. Mill, 1878: 578, 579).

Likewise, A. Marshall perceives education as a national investment, related to the needs of the labour force, as a contribution to the improvement of the productivity of labour and the enhancement of the economic efficiency of the large corporation. For him, the wisdom of expending public and private funds on education lies in its direct and indirect effects. Apart from the specialised training required for the special purposes of individual trades, a good education also confers great indirect benefits even on the ordinary workman: "It stimulates his mental activity; it fosters in him a habit of wise inquisitiveness"; and "it makes him more intelligent, more ready, more trustworthy in his ordinary work", thereby becoming "an important means towards the production of material wealth" (Marshall, 1920 [1890]: 207–216).

The underlying assumption in all these classical views is the retention of the classical notion of labour, perceived either as the 'people' or as the 'labouring classes', as a capacity to do manual work. This homogeneous perception of labour was modified by the contemporary human capital analysts on the ground that skills tend to differentiate labour, thereby making it heterogeneous. As Thurow puts it, labour "is no longer regarded as a homogeneous, fixed commodity, but as a commodity that may be expanded and improved" (Thurow, 1970: 11).

This means that the productivity of labour becomes a variable entity modified by individual decisions and public policy as regards the production of human capital. In this process, real skills and knowledge are acquired through formal and informal education and training. Thus the school becomes an educational institution specialising in the production of training (Schultz, 1961; Thurow, 1970; Becker, 1975; Blaug, 1992)[1].

These are the 'market benefits' of education and training implying that increases in the human skills, talents and knowledge (which are themselves sources of economic development), reinforced by a market-oriented and thus utilitarian perception of education[2], tend to condition the direction and the content of education not only in vocational schools but also in universities. Here, we have a growing concern with economic sustenance, that is, a concern with the reproduction of the skilled and knowledgeable individuals directed to the labour market. This kind of vocationalism tends to create such an understanding of work as to make the economy a priority in all types and phases of education. This is certainly a technocratic approach to education wherein education is seen as the outcome of economic and technological progress, and a mechanism for meeting the needs of the labour market (cf. Donald, 1992; Chisholm, 1992; Thurow, 1970). I shall argue in this work that the education and training actions of the Community have been greatly conditioned by these very socio-economic priorities.

2.2 The Political Approach

The primacy of these socio-economic concerns tends to ignore or even undermine the socialisation function of education perceived as a means for the inculcation of definite values and attitudes, thereby elevating culture and civilisation, not for merely bettering labour for production. This is the idea of 'liberal education'[3] originated in the works of classical theorists, among whom J.J. Rousseau, J. Mill, and J.S. Mill have a prominent position. For Rousseau, education is by definition the 'art of forming men' in the sense of making them both 'men and citizens', which entails a process of preparing them both as workers and as citizens by giving them the qualities of 'manhood' and of 'citizenship'. The qualities of 'manhood' are defined by man's duty to himself and to his own interests, while those of 'citizenship' derive from his duty to society and to the interests of others. As to whether the primary aim of education is to make a 'good man' or a 'good citizen', Rousseau is inclined towards the qualities of 'good citizenship'. In this sense education, called public or national education, aims at the welfare of the community by enhancing the 'general interest', the 'common good', without of course ignoring the 'private interests', the 'individual good'. This is so, Rousseau argues, because "the common element of these different interests is what forms the social tie", while the "general will alone can direct the state according to the object for which it was instituted, i.e. the common good" (Rousseau, 1966 [1762]: 20; Rousseau, 1979 [1762]; Boyd, 1911).

The interplay between 'individual interest' and 'common good' conditions the reasoning of J. Mill as well, for whom the end of education is to render the individual an instrument of happiness, first to himself ('personal happiness') and next to other beings ('the happiness of others'). In congruity with the utilitarian ideal, 'the greatest happiness of the greatest number of people', J. Mill's individualism requires that all men must be 'equally educated' in order to pursue their 'personal happiness', while the state becomes the 'active educator' of the community 'as to where true happiness lies'. Thus, notwithstanding that the strength of the domestic (parental) and the technical or scholastic education depends almost entirely upon the 'social', for 'society is the institutor', the nature of the 'social' depends almost entirely upon the 'political'. This implies that the means by which 'the grand objects of desire' may be attained, depend almost wholly upon 'the political machine', the state where interests are represented. The pursuit of general happiness comes, therefore, because the system of representation ensures it as the result of each pursuing his own interests. People though will know their own interests only by being educated, and this is how happiness comes about (J. Mill, 1992 [1823]; Burston, 1973).

In the same spirit, J.S. Mill argues that one of the most 'sacred duties' of the parents is to give to their children an education preparing them to perform their part well in life 'towards others and towards themselves'. But if the parents fail to fulfil this obligation, then the state 'ought to see it fulfilled', at the charge, as far as possible, of the parents. This idea of limited state intervention in education derives from the very principle of 'liberal education'. This is founded on the notion of 'individuality', itself considered to be 'the single most important ingredient in human well-being'. This 'individuality' is a constituent part of the qualities of 'good citizenship', reinforced by education in a liberal system of representative government (J.S. Mill, 1991 [1859]).

In the 'liberal education' tradition, therefore, the main function of education is not simply to give people skills for the pursuit of a particular profession, but primarily to train citizens so as to enhance political legitimisation. In the broader sense of learning and self-improvement, the education of citizens becomes an element conducive to social cohesion. This is because the education of citizens is thought to be a prerequisite to social and political emancipation and thus to the establishment of a democratic political system, the system of representative government. In this system, the function of education is perceived as a fundamental precondition for the true development of both the economic relations in the market and the political relations amongst social classes within the political system itself. For the liberal thinkers, the true representation of interests presupposes that all the citizens, including the workers themselves, have not only the right but also the ability to participate in the political process, and this ability is to a large extent conditioned by education itself. I shall argue in this work that 'citizenship' formation and broader 'liberal education' objectives, themselves considered to be a national responsibility, play a residual role in the education actions of the EU, thereby undermining the process of European political integration itself.

More than this, encircled by their ideological dispositions, the EU policy makers fail to appreciate the magnitude of idealisation contained in the notion of 'public good' or 'general interest' upon which both the 'utilitarian education' assumptions of 'human capital' and the 'liberal education' premises rest. For, after all, the state is not politically neutral and the education system, whether public or private, does contribute to political socialisation, meaning "the process through which values, cognitions and symbols are learned and internalised, through which operative social norms regarding politics are implanted, political consensus created, either effectively or ineffectively" (Eckestein and Apter, 1963 quoted in Miliband, 1974: 164). Miliband goes even further to argue that "educational institutions at all levels generally fulfil an important conservative role and act, with greater or lesser effectiveness, as legitimating agencies in and for their societies" (Miliband, 1974: 214).

This position is informed by Marx's thesis on the content and the role of ideas in society according to which "the ideas of the ruling class are in every epoch the ruling ideas, i.e. the class which is the ruling material force of society is at the same time its ruling intellectual force", which simply means that: "The class which has the means of material production at its disposal, has control at the same time over the means of mental production, so that thereby, generally speaking, the ideas of those who lack the means of mental production are subject to it" (Marx, 1977 [1846]: 176).

The underlying idea here is that the state ('ruling class') is dialectically related to the economy ('material production') and with the reproduction of ideas in society ('mental production'). This is in fact a process of reproduction of social relations, which defines the state-education relationship, and which entails the reproduction of (i) the relations of production by fostering capital accumulation, and (ii) the relations of domination by enhancing political legitimisation[4].

The former, within which the 'human capital' approach is now better understood, implies that the state (and the educational apparatus associated with it) aims at the reproduction of the division of labour and of the skills carried out under capitalism. The reproduction of knowledge and skills, therefore, constitutes one of the main objectives of the state and defines the social-economic dimension of education. The point here is that this reproduction primarily takes place outside the capitalist corporation. As Althusser put it, in a capitalist regime, unlike social formations characterised by slavery or serfdom, the reproduction of the skills of labour power "is achieved more and more outside production: by the capitalist education system, and by other instances and institutions" (Althusser, 1971: 132)[5]. It comes as no surprise, therefore, that the EU education and training initiatives, undertaken under the force of the imperatives of European **economic** integration, are primarily directed towards the reproduction of human capital in the form of knowledge residing in the specialised skills and abilities of labour itself.

The political legitimisation function, on the other hand, within which 'liberal education' thinking is understood as well, implies that one of the main aims of schooling is the legitimisation of the existing, or more emerging, social and political order. Here the state, through its ideological and educational apparatuses, operates as 'educator' by virtue of its hegemony exerted by the ruling class and organised by the intellectuals who are experts in legitimation. In this context, the schooling system becomes, as Torres put it, "a privileged instrument of socialisation for the hegemonic culture" (Torres, 1985: 4794)[6]. This being so, it now makes sense as to why, under the force of the uncertainties of European **political** integration, the socialisation function of education (expressed in EU language as 'the content of teaching and the organisation of education systems') continues to represent a prime national responsibility. The analysis which follows, starting with a presentation of the EU framework on education and training, will substantiate the main positions advanced above.

Notes

1 Mincer emphatically argues that the central idea of the human capital approach is that "human capacities are in large part acquired and developed through informal and formal education at home and at school, and through training, experience, and mobility in the labor market" (Mincer, 1992: 186. See also Mitch, 1992).

2 Human capital analysts argue that economic agents are utility maximisers and that education, as Johnes put it, "exists because it provides utility" (Johnes, 1993: 5).

3 For a definition of the concept 'liberal education' see, for instance, Schofield, 1972, ch.8.

4 For a review article on the state-education relationship in Marxist theory see Torres, 1985.

5 See also Torres, 1985; Bowles and Gintis, 1975 and 1976; O'Connor, 1973; Ringer, 1979. Arnove et al (1996) remind us that the education system may function "to perpetuate the social division of labor", but "it also can equip individuals with the skills and knowledge to humanize the work place and change the class structure of a society" (p.142).

6 See also Entwistle, 1979; Bowles and Gintis, 1976; Barker, 1990; Beetham, 1991; and Arnove et al (1996) who argue, along with Gramsci, that education is an agency not only "for achieving ideological consensus in a society" in accordance with "the norms and values of the dominant groups", but also for enabling 'subaltern groups' to develop "their own intellectuals and their own world views", thereby challenging "the existing interpretations of society by those in power" (p.142).

3 The EU Framework

The field of education and training in the EU has been defined by (i) the relevant provisions of the founding treaties, (ii) the European Court decisions on education and training, (iii) the legislative binding rules, and (iv) the executive non-binding acts of the Community concerning education and training.

3.1 Treaty Provisions

The treaties mainly define a process of economic integration centred on the establishment of a common market. Thus education and training in the treaties is a factor directed towards the fulfilment of this specific goal, the development and regulation of a Community labour market conducive to economic development in an enlarged economic area. It came as no surprise, therefore, that at least up to the European Union Treaty (1992) the field of education and training in the Community had been confined to a one-sided, economically-oriented perspective (Lenaerts, 1994). Here, the main objective had been the advancement of vocational training.

The notion of vocational training has a double meaning in the treaties. It means, firstly, an 'education process' directed towards an **existing** labour market, with the aim of creating, altering, or improving skills in the part of the surplus labour, the unemployed. Whether the treaties refer to the agricultural sector or to the sector of coal and steel or even to the entire economy, the main concern here is obvious: it is the economic crisis which produces unemployment and reinforces not only the economic rationalisation of production through the introduction of new technologies and methods of production, but also the improvement of the accessibility of the labour force as well as the productivity of labour through the vocational training and retraining of those of the workers who either have low skills or are being forced to change work.

The second meaning of the notion of vocational training refers to the education process which directs itself to **prospective** members of the labour force, i.e. the youth who are in a process of transition from school to adult and working life. The objective here is to provide the young people with skills and knowledge suitable for a changing economy and society, under the impact of the new technologies, the information technologies. It is in this context that provisions of the treaties refer not only to advanced vocational training, but also to the need for the Community and the member states to promote cooperation between research centres and universities, and to stimulate the training and mobility of students, teachers and researchers in the Community.

This is a call for the member states and the Community to act not only in the area of vocational training, but also in that of education itself, whether formal or informal. The EEC Treaty, however, granted no competence to the Community to develop a policy in the field of education. This competence, albeit within specified limits, was given to the Community through the EU Treaty, with the aim of contributing to the development of quality education, irrespective of the vocational aim of the education (Lenaerts, 1994).

In spite of the absence of clear education provisions in the EEC Treaty, the Community did act in the past in this field, not only with non-binding 'conclusions' or 'resolutions' of the Council and the Ministers of Education meeting within the Council, but also with binding rules in the form of 'regulations', 'directives' or 'decisions'. This became possible, as indicated below, only with the help of the European Court of Justice through its interpretations which made more flexible the boundaries between education and vocational training.

Exhibit 3.1: Treaty provisions on education and training

1 **ECSC Treaty**

   Article 56: If fundamental changes in market conditions or the introduction of new technical processes should lead to a large reduction in labour requirements in the coal and steel industry, the Community may provide non repayable aid towards the financing of vocational training for workers having to change their employment.

2 **EEC Treaty**

   Article 41: To enable the objectives of the common agricultural policy (CAP) to be attained, provision may be made within the framework of the CAP for measures such as: an effective coordination of efforts in the spheres of vocational training, of research and of the dissemination of agricultural knowledge.

Article 57: In order to make it easier for persons to take up and pursue activities as self-employed persons, the Community shall issue directives for the mutual recognition of diplomas, certificates and other evidence of formal qualifications.

Article 118: The Community shall have the task of promoting close cooperation between member states in the social field, including matters relating to basic and advanced vocational training.

Articles 123,125: A European Social Fund is established with the task of rendering the employment of workers easier and of increasing their geographical and occupational mobility within the Community, in particular through vocational training of unemployed workers (The EU Treaty made the following addition to Art. 123: 'to facilitate their adaptation to industrial changes and to changes in production systems, in particular through vocational training and retraining').

Article 128: The Community shall lay down general principles of implementing a common vocational training policy capable of contributing to the harmonious development both of the national economies and of the common market.

3   EAEC Treaty (Euratom)

Article 9: An institution of university status shall be established, and the Community may set up schools for the training of specialists, particularly in the fields of prospecting for minerals, the production of high-purity nuclear materials, the processing of irradicated fuels, nuclear engineering, health and safety and the production and use of radioisotopes.

4   SEA

Article 130g: In pursuing the objective of strengthening the scientific and technological bases of EC industry, the Community shall carry out activities such as (i) the implementation of research, technological development and demonstration programmes, by promoting cooperation with and between undertakings, research centres and universities; and (ii) the stimulation of the training and mobility of researchers in the Community.

5   EU Treaty

Article 126: The Community shall contribute to the development of quality education by encouraging cooperation between member states and, if necessary, by supporting and supplementing their action, while fully respecting the responsibility of the member states for the content of teaching and the organisation of education systems and their cultural and linguistic diversity.

Community action shall be aimed at (i) developing the European dimension in education, particularly through the teaching and dissemination of the languages of the member states; (ii) encouraging mobility of students and teachers, inter alia by encouraging the academic recognition of diplomas and periods of study; (iii) promoting cooperation between educational establishments; (iv) developing exchanges of information and experience on issues common to the education systems of the member states; (v) encouraging the development of youth exchanges and of exchanges of socio-educational instructors; and (vi) encouraging the development of distance education.

Article 127: The Community shall implement a vocational training policy which shall support and supplement the action of the member states, while fully respecting the responsibility of the member states for the content and organisation of vocational training.

Community action shall aim to (i) facilitate adaptation to industrial changes, in particular through vocational training and retraining; (ii) improve initial and continuing vocational training in order to facilitate vocational integration and reintegration into the labour market; (iii) facilitate access to vocational training and encourage mobility of instructors and trainees and particularly young people; (iv) stimulate cooperation on training between educational or training establishments and firms; and (v) develop exchanges of information and experience on issues common to the training systems of the member states.

Article 3b: In areas which do not fall within its exclusive competence, the Community shall take action, in accordance with the principle of subsidiarity, only if the objectives of the proposed action cannot be sufficiently achieved by the member states and can therefore be better achieved by the Community.

3.2 European Court Decisions

The Court decisions on education and training are mainly based on the provisions of the Treaties on the free movement of persons, the mobility of labour, the improvement of the living standards of workers, and the principle of non-discrimination between nationals of member states of the Community. The Court's objective appears to be the expansion of the notion of vocational training, within of course the limits imposed by the treaties, thereby broadening the Community jurisdiction on education and training, and the safeguarding of non-discriminatory treatment of Community nationals, thereby making equal the access to educational courses and the labour market.

The objective to expand the notion of vocational training initially came through a broad definition by which any form of education, which either prepares for a particular 'profession, trade or employment' or provides the necessary skills for such a 'profession, trade or employment', is vocational training. This holds true irrespective of the level of training and the age of the students, and even if the training programme includes 'an element of general education'.

Thus the ground was prepared for the inclusion of university studies into the confines of vocational training. For the purposes of Community law, it became possible to regard university studies preparatory to the exercise of a trade or a profession as being covered by the term 'vocational training'. It is true that in Universities there are certain programmes and courses of study which, because of their particular nature, are intended for persons wishing to improve their general knowledge rather than to prepare themselves for an occupation. But in general, in the Court's opinion, university studies fulfil the criteria set up in the definition of vocational training, even if the studies include an element of general education. In this last case, according to the judgment of the Court, university education must be regarded as a single unit wherein it is not possible to make a distinction between one part which does not constitute vocational training and another which does: the various years of a study programme cannot be assessed individually but must be considered within the framework of the programme as a whole, particularly in the light of the programme's purpose, which in university studies is generally to prepare for a qualification for a particular profession.

As to the Court's objective to uphold the principle of non-discrimination among Community nationals, the decision on the recognition of diplomas was to make the evaluation of a professional qualification part of the Community legal practice as defined by the provisions on the freedom of movement of workers and of establishment. Thus a decision by any member state refusing to recognise the equivalence of a diploma granted to a migrant worker by the state of origin can be made the subject of judicial proceedings under Community law, while a similar decision on a national diploma whose holder desires to exercise a professional activity in another member state can constitute a restriction incompatible with the freedom of establishment.

In the same context of non-discrimination, the Court's decisions aim at creating conditions of equal access to educational courses. Thus the student's right of residence for vocational training purposes is upheld. Also, the stipulation of an enrolment fee applicable only to students of another member state, in order to make them eligible to take part in educational courses, is considered an act constituting discrimination by reason of nationality. Likewise, the Court upheld the right of the children of migrant workers to be admitted to educational courses under the same conditions as the nationals of the host state, and this refers not only to admission requirements, but also to general measures intended to facilitate educational attendance.

Exhibit 3.2: European Court decisions on education and training

1 On vocational training

Case 293/83: Gravier vs City of Liege, [1985] *European Court Reports (ECR)* 593, defines vocational training as any form of education which prepares for a qualification for a particular profession.

Case 24/86: Blaizot vs University of Liege, [1988] ECR 379, reaffirms the previous definition of vocational training and adds that university studies constitute as well vocational training not only where the final academic examination directly provides the required qualification for a particular profession, but also in so far as the studies in question provide specific training and skills needed by the student for the pursuit of a profession.

Case 242/87: Commission vs Council, [1989] ECR 1425, reaffirms the previous definition whereby any form of education which prepares for a qualification for a particular profession is vocational training, and adds that this holds even if the training programme includes an element of general education. In this context, the Court states, the Community Erasmus programme concerns mainly the sphere of vocational training and that of scientific research, the latter being characteristically one of the proper functions of a university, while preparing students for a profession.

Joined Cases C-51/89, C-90/89 and C-94/89: UK and others vs Council, [1991] ECR I-2757, reaffirm the previous definition on vocational training and add that the Community programme Comett seeks to ensure intra-Community cooperation between universities and industry regarding initial and continuing training in advanced technology, and that in keeping with Community law there can be no distinction between initial training and continuing training.

Case 263/86: Belgium vs Humbel, [1988] ECR 5365, defines education as a whole in the sense that the various years of a study programme cannot be assessed individually but must be considered within the framework of the programme as a whole. And this because the programme forms a coherent single entity and cannot be divided into two parts, one of which does not constitute vocational training while the other does. Thus, in the case of university education (see Case 242/87, op. cit.), studies may be divided into different stages but must be regarded as a single unit wherein it is not possible to make a distinction between one stage which does not constitute vocational training and a second which does.

2   On the recognition of diplomas

Case 71/76: Thieffry vs Conseil de l'ordre des avocats a la Cour de Paris, [1977] ECR 765, makes a distinction between academic effect and the civil effect of the recognition of equivalence of foreign diplomas, and states that the fact that a national legislation provides for recognition of equivalence only for university purposes does not of itself justify the refusal to recognise such equivalence as evidence of a professional qualification. Such a refusal, the Court states, would be a restriction incompatible with the freedom of establishment guaranteed by Community law.

Case 222/86: Unectef vs Heylens, [1989]1 ECLR 901, deals with migrant workers and states that where access to an occupation as an employed person is dependent upon the possession of a diploma , then a decision refusing to recognise the equivalence of a diploma granted to a worker by the member-state of origin can be made the subject of judicial proceedings in which its legality under Community law can be reviewed.

3   On students and migrant workers' children

Case C-295/90: Parliament vs Council, [1992] ECR I-4193, refers to a student's right of residence for vocational training purposes and states that the principle of non-discrimination with regard to the conditions of access to vocational training implies that a national of a member state, who has been admitted to a vocational training course in another member state, enjoys a right of residence for the duration of the course.

Case 152/82: Forcheri vs Belgium, [1983] ECR 2323, refers to migrant workers and states that if a member state organises educational courses relating in particular to vocational training, to require of a national of another member state lawfully established in the first member state an enrolment fee which is not required of its own nationals in order to take part in such courses constitutes discrimination by reason of nationality, which is prohibited by Article 7 of the Community Treaty.

Case 39/86: Lair vs Universität Hannover, [1988] ECR 3161, states that a national of another member state who undertakes university studies in the host state leading to a professional qualification, after having engaged in occupational activity in that state, must be regarded as having retained his status as a worker and is entitled as such to the social benefit of Article 7(2) of Regulation no1612/68 on freedom of movement of workers within the Community, provided that there is a link between the previous occupational activity and the studies in question.

Case 197/86: Brown vs Scotland, [1988] ECR 3205, refers to migrant workers and states that if such a worker enters into an employment relationship for a period of eight months with a view to subsequently undertaking studies in the host state in the same field of activity and who would not have been employed by his employer if he had not already been accepted for admission to university is to be regarded as a worker but is not entitled to receive for the purposes of his studies an allowance payable to students who are nationals of the host state in respect of their maintenance.

Case 235/87: Matteucci vs Belgium, [1989]1 CMLR 357, refers to migrant workers and states that Community law does not allow the authorities of a member state to refuse to grant a scholarship to pursue studies in another member state on the grounds that the worker does not have the nationality of the member state of residence.

Case 293/83: Gravier vs City of Liege, [1985] ECR 593, states that the imposition on students, who are nationals of other member states, of a charge, a registration fee or the so-called 'minerval' as a condition of access to vocational training, where the same fee is not imposed on students who are nationals of the host member state, constitutes discrimination on grounds of nationality contrary to Article 7 of the Community Treaty (See also Case 24/86: Blaizot vs University of Liege, [1988] ECR 337, on the same question).

Case 9/74: Casagrande vs Munchen, [1974] ECR 773, states that migrant workers' children shall be admitted to educational courses under the same conditions as the nationals of the host state as regards both admission and the general measures intended to facilitate educational attendance.

> **Joined Cases 389 and 390/87:** Echternach and Moritz vs Netherlands, [1989] ECR 723, refers to migrant workers' children and states that (i) the child of such a worker retains the status of member of the worker's family when that child's family returns to the host state in order to continue his studies, and (ii) assistance granted to cover the costs of student's education and maintenance is to be regarded as a social advantage to which the children of Community workers are entitled under the same conditions as apply to the host country's own nationals.

These decisions of the Court had been reinforced by specific legislative binding rules of the Community on such issues as cooperation in education, vocational training, recognition of academic and professional qualifications, and access to educational courses by nationals of another member state and by the migrant workers' children. It is to these questions that we now turn.

3.3   Legislative Binding Rules

3.3.1 Education of migrants' children

In dealing with the education of the children of migrant workers, the Community wanted to facilitate the free movement of workers within its territory. Migrant workers were thought to be not only those of the workers who came from a non-Community country, but also the nationals of a member state who were employed in another member state. However, the binding rules of the Community on this matter deal exclusively with Community nationals and their children, while for the children of migrant workers originating from non-Community countries the member states and the Community organs restricted themselves to only non-binding acts.

Regulation 68/1612 enables the children of Community migrant workers to be admitted to educational courses under the same conditions as the nationals of the host state, and asks the member states to encourage all efforts conducive to the attendance of these courses under the best possible conditions. Similarly, Directive 77/486 requires the member states to take appropriate measures to ensure that 'free tuition to facilitate initial reception' is offered in their territory to the migrant children, for whom school attendance is compulsory under the laws of the host state, including the teaching of the official language of the host state, as well as the training and further training of the teachers who are to provide the tuition. In addition, the host state must take the appropriate measures, in cooperation with the states of origin, to promote teaching for these children of the mother tongue and culture of the country of origin.

Exhibit 3.3: Legislative binding rules on the education of migrants' children

1 **Council Regulation 68/1612/EEC** of 15 October 1968 on freedom of movement of workers within the Community: OJL 257, 19. 10. 1968, stipulates that the children of a Community national who is employed in the territory of another member state must have access to the host state's general educational, apprenticeship and vocational training courses under the same conditions as the national of that state.

2 **Council Directive 77/486/EEC** of 25 July 1977 on the education of the children of migrant workers: OJL 199, 6. 8. 1977.

As for the children of migrant workers originating from non-member countries, the member states of the Community expressed their will to promote, for the benefit of the nations of the member states and of non-member countries, actions such as the study of the language or languages of the host country, the teaching if possible of the children's mother tongue and culture, and the exchange of information for families on the training and educational opportunities available to them[1]. This expressed will of the member states was also upheld by the European Parliament whose members collectively stressed the importance of such measures if effective equality was to be established for the citizens of the Community, wherever their place of residence and whatever their nationality of origin[2].

The problem does not seem to be of minor importance since, beyond the total number of non-nationals in member states' schools estimated at around 10 per cent of the total school population, the percentage of children affected by contact with speakers of languages other than their own is estimated to represent around 50 per cent of school children in member states [COM(94)80]. Yet, ten years after the introduction of the Directive on the education of the children of migrant workers, it was reported that the situation in several member states had not significantly changed regarding reception classes for immigrants, initial and further training for teachers responsible for reception education, and the teaching of the language and culture of origin. As a result, success rates among the children of migrants were still "too low and failure rates too high, making it difficult for these children to go on to further education and training" [COM(88)787, p.129]. A condition which inevitably tends to undermine not only the social cohesion of the societies of the Community, but also its central priority aimed to improve the conditions of freedom of movement for workers.

3.3.2 Recognition of qualifications

The concept of free movement is at the root of the functioning of the European area for the professions and training, for which recognition of qualifications for academic and professional purposes is the principal mode of action. The Community has dealt with this problem by using two differing approaches. One was the so-called 'sectoral approach' to the recognition of qualifications which implied for each profession coordination amongst the member states at Community level, prior to the recognition of diplomas or other qualifications. In the area of the skilled workers, the Community act on the comparability of vocational training qualifications aims at establishing general rules but also has elements of sectoral consideration. It calls for a common action by the member states and the Community to establish the comparability of vocational training qualifications as regards skilled workers in mutually agreed occupations or groups of occupations[3]. Likewise, the Community acts for certain liberal professions required from the member states to recognise, under certain conditions, the formal qualifications awarded to nationals of member states by the other member states, thereby giving them the right to take up and pursue the self-employed activities of their profession within the territory of the Community.

The requirements here were clear and specific: the duration and the level of the education and training governing access to those professions had to either be regulated in a similar fashion in all member states or be subject to a minimal harmonisation needed to establish sectoral systems for the mutual recognition of diplomas. For each profession, two directives were adopted: one for the coordination and the harmonisation of training as regards both the content and the duration of educational courses, and the other for the establishment of the automatic recognition of diplomas on the basis of the minimal Community standards imposed.

The other approach used by the Community was to provide not specific measures for every regulated profession, but instead a general system of recognition of qualifications. The Community measures fall into two categories here – one for those who have higher education diplomas awarded on completion of professional education and training of at least three years education, and the other for those who either have post-secondary education diplomas obtained after a period of less than three years and secondary education diplomas, or have not obtained diplomas but have acquired professional experience. The recognition of qualifications refers to regulated professional activity, and requires as pre-requisite the possession of a diploma or professional title based on certain qualifications.

These actions of the Community have been circumscribed not only by the unwillingness of the member states to release national jurisdiction over the organisation and the content of education, but also by the still unsettled tension between professional and academic recognition[4]. For, while the former is a way of establishing a single market defined by Community law offering each individual wider scope of employment in a given occupation, the latter aims to give a European dimension to education in each member state, thereby improving the quality of education in Community generally, but at the same time raising fences of national jurisdiction. The outcome cannot but be a further obstacle to the freedom of movement of persons.

Exhibit 3.4: Legislative binding rules on the recognition of qualifications

1 On general recognition

Council Decision 63/266/EEC of 2 April 1963 laying down general principles for implementing a common vocational training policy, and in particular the eighth principle which calls for a standardised description of the basic qualifications required at various levels of training and also harmonisation of the standards required for success in final examinations, with a view to the mutual recognition of certificates and other documents confirming completion of vocational training: OJ no 63, 20. 4. 1963, p1338/63.

Council Decision 85/368/EEC of 16 July 1985 on the comparability of vocational training qualifications in the member states: OJ L199, 31. 7. 1985.

Council Directive 89/48/EEC of 21 December 1988 on a general system for the recognition of higher education diplomas awarded on completion of professional education and training of at least three years duration: OJ L19, 24. 10. 1989.

Council Directive 92/51/EEC of 18 June 1992 on a second general system for the recognition of professional education and training (which complements Directive 89/48/EEC): OJ L209, 24. 7. 1992.

2   On sectoral recognition

Council Directives 75/362 and 75/363 on the mutual recognition of diplomas and the right of establishment for **doctors:** OJ L167, 30. 6. 1975.

Council Directives 77/452 and 77/453 on the mutual recognition...for **nurses:** OJ L176, 27. 6. 1977.

Council Directives 78/686 and 78/687 on the mutual recognition...for **dentists:** OJ L233, 25. 7. 1978.

Council Directives 78/1026 and 78/1027 on the mutual recognition...for **veterinary surgeons:** OJ L362, 18. 12. 1978.

Council Directives 80/154 and 80/155 on the mutual recognition...for **midwives:** OJ L33, 21. 1. 1980.

Council Directives 85/432 and 85/433 on the mutual recognition...for **pharmacists:** OJ L253, 16. 9. 1985.

Council Directive 85/384 for the mutual recognition.. for **architects:** OJ L223, 10. 6. 1985 (Also between 1964 and 1982, several directives were issued to ensure the mutual recognition of conditions for access to particular so-called traditional professions or occupations in such economic activities as personal services (in hotels, bars, restaurants), retail and wholesale trade, industry and crafts, insurance, transport etc).

3.3.3 Foreign language competence

The establishment of a single labour market in the Community is directly related to the ability of people to communicate. Lack of foreign language skills is thus the Achilles Heel in the Community-wide effort to make the free movement of persons and ideas a practical reality. In this sense not only the development of greater understanding among the peoples of the Community but also the effective exercise of their rights to free movement and freedom of establishment are dependent to a large extent on their ability to communicate through a second Community language

other than their mother tongue. It is for this reason that early education action proposals of the Community stressed the need for language
teaching from an early age in primary schools through the different
stages of education to higher and adult education[5].

In keeping with this conception the Community action programme on
foreign language competence (Lingua) identified five areas of cooperation and action. The first included measures to promote in-service training of foreign language teachers, defined as those whose regular activity
was to teach as a foreign language one or more languages at any level
of education or training other than university level. The objective here
was to make a Community contribution, with aid amounting annually
to a maximum of ECU 25,000, so as to improve the skills of communication of such teachers and trainers in the language concerned, to
encourage diversification in foreign language teaching and competence
in the least widely used and least taught languages, and also to help them
establish and develop the framework needed to organise educational
exchanges.

Learning of foreign languages in universities was the second area of
cooperation aimed at developing the initial training of foreign language
teachers. This implied Community-wide mobility and exchange of those
students specialising in foreign languages in conjunction with another
discipline.

The third area of cooperation dealt with the issue of foreign language-
learning as a means of improving access to the labour market,and called
for the introduction of measures to promote knowledge of foreign languages used in work relations and in economic life. The aim here was
to contribute to the development of teaching and learning of foreign languages as an essential component of vocational training of workers and
trainers, particularly in small and medium-sized enterprises.

The development of exchanges for young people undergoing professional, vocational and technical education within the Community was
the fourth area of cooperation. The issue here was support for the development of such exchanges, of a minimum duration of 14 days, organised as part of a project of an educational establishment. The aim of the
projects had to be the improvement of communication skills in foreign
languages and thus the motivation of those taking part to acquire competence in foreign languages.

Finally the programme provided for complementary support to the
educational structures of the member states so as to underpin the creation of a network of communication between structures, facilitating

cooperation between them and thus contributing to the promotion of foreign language competence in the Community.

These Community actions were designed to deal with two interrelated issues as regards foreign language competence: one was the issue of language-learning for vocational training purposes, and the other for broader education purposes. The first has now found expression in the Community 'Leonardo' programme which calls for cooperation with a view to improving language skills in cases of initial vocational training and the transition of young people to working life as well as continuing vocational training and lifelong learning. While the second is now expressed through the Community 'Socrates' programme which calls for the learning of the languages of the Community as an integral part of university studies, and also for the creation of multilateral or bilateral partnerships between schools with the aim of promoting the knowledge of Community languages, particularly those which are least widely used and least taught. In the context of these new programmes the Community hopes to improve the quality of language learning and teaching, and also to diversify the learning and teaching of the languages taught in the member states[6].

In its initial phase between 1 January 1990 and 31 December 1994, Lingua was a programme of actions for the quantitative and qualitative promotion of the Community languages taught or learned as foreign languages. The budget allocated for implementing the programme was estimated at ECU 200 million, and slightly more than ECU 153 million was in fact allocated. The experience of the programme clearly demonstrates that promoting of foreign language competence, in terms of both quantity and quality, is possible only within a coherent overall framework, which implies synergy between the different Community programme actions, including those designed for youth exchanges and for vocational training[7].

Exhibit 3.5: Legislative binding rules on foreign language competence

Council Decision 63/266/EEC of 2 April 1963 laying down general principles for implementing a common vocational training policy, and in particular the seventh principle which provides that the suitable training of teachers and instructors,whose numbers should be increased and whose technical and teaching skills should be developed, shall be one of the basic factors of any effective vocational training policy: OJ no 63, 20. 4. 1963, p1338/63.

Council Decision 89/489/EEC of 28 July 1989 establishing an action programme to promote foreign language competence in the European Community (Lingua): OJ L239, 16. 8. 1989.

Council Decision 94/819/EC of 6 December 1994 establishing an action programme for the implementation of a European Community vocational training policy ('Leonardo da Vinci programme'), and in particular the Strand III Community measure on support for the development of cooperation with a view to improving language skills: OJ L340, 29. 12. 1994.

Council and Parliament Decision 95/819/EC of 14 March 1995 establishing the Community action programme 'Socrates', and in particular the provisions on the promotion of language skills in the Community which includes the learning of the languages of the European Union as an integral part of studies, with emphasis on the least widely used and least taught languages: OJ L87, 20 April 1995.

3.3.4 Youth exchanges and mobility

The actions of the Community on youth exchanges and mobility are basically aimed to contribute to vocational youth training through the exchange of young workers within the Community, and also to educational youth training through the exchange of young persons not necessarily young workers. In both cases the common objective has been to provide valuable preparation conducive to the achievement of the removal of obstacles to the free movement of persons, and also to contribute to the training and preparation of young people for adult and working life. This means that the promotion of youth exchanges and of young workers is considered to be an appropriate method for improving understanding among young people and becoming better acquainted with the diverse cultures of the member states, thereby helping to strengthen democracy, tolerance and cohesion in the Community.

The Community action programme on the exchange of young workers underlines the need for greater opportunities to be offered to young workers, aged from 18 to 28 years, in order to broaden their vocational training and their cultural, linguistic and human knowledge in a member state other than that in which they reside. Under the plan, eligible young workers are those who are employed or are available in the labour market, in accordance with national legislation and practice, and have already received basic vocational training or have practical working experience. These young workers may choose training periods of either long duration, being of a predominantly vocational nature and lasting between 4 and 16 months with an employer in the host country, or short duration in the form of a study training period lasting between 3 weeks and 3 months and designed to enable participants to establish close contact with the working and living environment of the host country.

A Community survey conducted for the period 1985–1991 indicates a large satisfaction of the participants in the exchange. A quarter of them took part in the exchange immediately after having finished vocational training, while approximately half had already worked for a few years. However, only a third of the participants stated the desire to develop their professional knowledge as their primary motivation for taking part. Instead, decisive factors were their desire to know another European country and to improve foreign language skills. Thus, according to the Community report, the exchange programme in question seems to be a perfectly good model if used as a 'first introduction' to various aspects, including professional ones, of another country, whereas longer project models are better suited for training and improvement of professional skills [COM(92)512 final].

The 'Youth for Europe' programme has similar stipulations and objectives and refers to bilateral or multilateral exchanges arranged on the basis of joint plans between groups of young people, between the ages of 15 and 25 years, of a minimum duration of one week in a member state other than that in which they reside. The main aim of the programme has been to enable the young people to develop skills for active and working life by gaining an understanding of the economic, social and cultural life of the host country and by establishing cooperative relationships between groups of young people resident in different member states, thus strengthening their awareness of belonging to Europe. In its third phase, the programme stresses the importance of enabling young people to become aware of the value of democracy in the organisation of society, and also to view the Community as an integral part of their historical, cultural and social environment.

Community reports on the evaluation of the programme, following its initial application, indicate that the programme has generally generated a good deal of enthusiasm among young people in all the member states. In 1993, for example, about 40,000 young people benefited directly from the programme. In qualitative terms, having an explicitly educational purpose, the programme stimulated ongoing links between participants and developed young people's awareness of the European dimension [COM(95)159 final][8]. This last issue tends to define Community action in both education and vocational training.

Exhibit 3.6: Legislative binding rules on youth exchanges in the Community

Council Decision 79/642/EEC of 16 July 1979 establishing a second joint programme to encourage the exchange of young workers within the Community: OJ L185, 21. 7. 1979 (established following the experience gained in the implementation of the first joint programme adopted on 8 May 1964 by the representatives of the Governments of the member states of the EEC meeting within the Council: OJ No78, 22. 5. 1964, p1226/64).

Council Decision 84/636/EEC of 13 December1984 establishing a third joint programme to encourage the exchange of young workers within the Community: OJ L331, 19. 12. 1984, as amended by **Council Decision 90/268/EEC** of 29 May 1990: OJ L156, 21. 6. 1990.

Council Decision 88/348/EEC of 16 June 1988 adopting an action programme for the promotion of youth exchanges in the Community – 'Youth for Europe' programme (1988–1991): OJ L158, 25. 6. 1988.

Council Decision 91/395/EEC of 29 July 1991 adopting the 'Youth for Europe' programme (second phase:1992–1994): OJ L217, 6. 8. 1991.

Council and Parliament Decision 95/818/EC of 14 March 1995 adopting the third phase of the 'Youth for Europe' programme (1995–1999): OJ L87, 20. 4. 1995.

3.3.5 Vocational training

The Community measures on vocational training include several inter-related themes such as the information and guidance, the continuing vocational training, the advanced vocational training for technology, and the vocational education and initial training of young people and their preparation for adult and working life.

The establishment of a European Centre for the Development of Vocational Training, called in brief 'Cedefop', was thought to be the appropriate means for an effective implementation of a common vocational training policy in the Community. Although the general principles for implementing such a policy were laid down in the early 1960s, the Centre was established in the mid-1970s, following the agreement among the member states on a social action programme aimed at a common vocational training policy[9].

The aim of the Centre, whose seat was initially in Berlin and later (1994) moved to Thessaloniki (Greece), has been the promotion and development of vocational training and in-service training, mainly through its scientific and technical activities, the exchange of information and the comparison of experience, and the approximation of standards of vocational training with a view to the mutual recognition of certificates and other documents attesting completion of vocational training.

Of the many forms, initial vocational training is one which enables young people to make easier the transition from school to working life. In this regard, the Community felt the need to give a European dimension to the various training initiatives by ensuring that young people could receive one year's, or if possible two or more years', initial vocational training, in addition to their full-time compulsory education, leading to a recognised vocational qualification. The Petra programme, which was introduced for this specific purpose, defines initial vocational training as 'any form of initial vocational training of non-university level', including 'technical vocational training and apprenticeship', which 'enables young people to gain a vocational qualification' recognised by the competent authorities of the member states concerned. The point is reiterated in the Community Charter of the fundamental social rights of workers wherein the heads of the member states took the position that, following the end of compulsory education, young people 'must be entitled to receive initial vocational training of a sufficient duration to enable them to adapt to the requirements of their future working life'[10].

The rationale of these Community actions has been to improve the quality of education and training, and equality of opportunity, for all young people, and also to grapple with young people's preparation for working life and their progression from school to training, work and adulthood in a European context and through joint Community initiatives[11].

In the current epoch of the new information technology,this transition from school to working life requires advanced vocational training and thus closer cooperation between universities and enterprises. The Community measures (cf. Comett programme) on this question purport to give a European dimension to cooperation between universities and enterprises in training relating to innovation and the development and application of new technologies. In this way the Community aims at improving the supply of training at local, regional and national level and thus contributing to the balanced economic development of the Community. The main objective is to foster the joint development of training programmes and the exchange of experience, and also the optimum use of training resources at Community level, notably through the creation of transnational sectoral and regional networks of advanced technology training projects.

The underlying concern is the ongoing restructuring changes in the technological and industrial spheres and their impact on the competitiveness of Community industry. These changes create a need for in-service vocational training schemes, in the context of regional cooperation between industry and higher education sectors, thereby contributing to the development of highly skilled human resources[12].

This need for permanent adaptation to the changing nature and content of occupations has made imperative the 'continuing vocational training', implying any vocational training engaged in by a worker throughout his working life. The Community measures (cf. Force programme) on this issue are aimed to facilitate constant adaptation to new demands, to enable the least qualified workers to benefit from continuing vocational training, to advance effective equality of opportunity for men and women regarding access to continuing vocational training, to give appropriate attention to the vocational needs of disabled people and the promotion of their social integration and independent way of life, to make national officials aware of the Community dimension of their work, and above all to promote the European dimension in continuing vocational training in order to improve the conditions for workers' mobility.

The underlying principle in this endeavour is again the economic and social necessity of the Community wherein the completion of the internal market must go hand in hand with improved access to vocational training. This means that vocational training and management of human resources are decisive factors in the adaptation of undertakings and their capacity to respond to change. More specifically, factors such as the acceleration of economic, industrial and technical change, in an international conjuncture of increased competition, coupled with the advent of the completion of the internal market, demand reinforcement of the anticipatory and adaptational role played by continuing vocational training[13].

All the preceding Community measures on vocational training have now found expression, following the Treaty on European Union, in the Leonardo programme designed to advance the implementation of a Community vocational training policy. The programme is based on the realisation that Community cooperation on vocational training has so far brought a genuine added value to the actions undertaken in and by member states. This allows for the development of a global and coherent approach towards vocational training in the sense of rationalising the action programmes in the vocational training field into a single programme, which focuses on defining objectives, while leaving member states free to choose the means appropriate to their situation.

The programme provides support for improving the vocational training systems and arrangements in the member states as well as the vocational training measures, including university/industry cooperation, with regard to undertakings and workers, and also for developing linguistic competence and the knowledge and dissemination of innovations in the sphere of vocational training. This effort to develop a European dimension in vocational training is based on the assumption that there is an imperative need in the Community to improve the quality of vocational training in the member states, in order to encourage continuing opportunities for individuals to improve their knowledge and skills, and thus contribute to increased economic and social cohesion as well as to the competitiveness of the European economies[14]. The approach here is such as to ensure overall consistency between the vocational training programme and the Community actions in the field of education proper, which, as indicated below, has a long history in Community involvement and member-states cooperation.

Exhibit 3.7: Legislative binding rules on vocational training

1   On information and guidance

Council Regulation 75/337/EEC of 10 February 1975 establishing a European Centre for the Development of Vocational Training(Cedefop): OJ L39, 13. 2. 1975, as amended by **Council Regulation 94/1131/EC** of 16 May 1994: OJ L127, 19. 5. 1994, and **Council Regulation 95/251/EC** of 6 February 1995: OJ L30, 9. 2. 1995.

2   On continuing vocational training

Council Directive 76/207/EEC of 9 February 1976 on the implementation of the principle of equal treatment for men and women as regards access to employment, vocational training and promotion, and working conditions: OJ L39, 14. 1. 1976 (cf. the Iris network on vocational training for women: OJ L342/35, 4. 12. 1987).

Council Decision 88/231/EEC of 18 April 1988 establishing a second Community action programme for disabled people (Helios): OJ L104/38, 23. 4. 1988.

Council Decision 90/267/EEC of 29 May 1990 establishing an action programme for the development of continuing vocational training in the European Community (Force): OJ L156, 21. 6. 1990.

Council Decision 91/341/EEC of 20 June 1991 adopting a Community action programme for the vocational training of customs officials (Matthaeus programme): OJ L187, 13. 7. 1991.

Council Decision 92/481/EEC of 22 September 1992 adopting an action plan for the exchange between member state administrations of national officials engaged in the implementation of Community legislation required to achieve the internal market: OJ L286, 1. 10. 1992.

Council Decision 93/588/EEC of 29 October 1993 adopting a Community action programme on the vocational training of indirect taxation officials (Matthaeus-tax programme): OJ L280, 13. 11. 1993.

3 On advanced vocational training

Council Decision 86/365/EEC of 24 July 1986 adopting the Community action programme for education and training for technology (COMETT): OJ L222, 8 August 1986.

Council Decision 89/27/EEC of 16 December 1988 adopting the second phase of the programme on cooperation between universities and industry regarding training in the field of technology (COMETT II, 1990–1994): OJ L13, 17. 1. 1989.

Council Decision 89/657/EEC of 18 December 1989 establishing an action programme to promote innovation in the field of vocational training resulting from technological change in the European Community (Eurotecnet): OJ L393, 31. 12. 1989.

4 On vocational education and initial training

Council Decision 87/569/EEC of 1 December 1987 concerning an action programme for the vocational training of young people and their preparation for adult and working life (PETRA): OJ L346, 10. 12. 1987, as amended by **Council Decision 91/387/EEC** of 22 July 1991: OJ L214, 2. 8. 1991.

---

5   On vocational training in general

Council Decision 63/266/EEC of 2 April 1963 laying down general principles for implementing a common vocational training policy: OJ No63, 20. 4. 1963.

Council Decision 94/819/EC of 6 December 1994 establishing an action programme for the implementation of a European Community vocational training policy ('Leonardo da Vinci programme'): OJ L340, 29. 12. 1994.

3.3.6 Cooperation in education

In the mid-1970s the Ministers for Education, meeting within the Council, stressed the need to institute European cooperation in the field of education on the principle that such cooperation, while reflecting the progressive harmonisation of the economic and social policies in the Community, had to be adapted to the specific requirements and objectives of this field, taking into consideration the fact that education on no account could be regarded merely as a component of economic life[15].

This common position led to a Community action programme in the field of education centred on the following main considerations: firstly, to create better facilities in the member states for the education and training of nationals and the children of nationals of other member states and of no-member countries; secondly, to improve mutual understanding of the various educational systems by promoting closer relations between them and thus bringing existing information on education to the attention of the citizens of the Community; thirdly, to promote and organise study visits and exchanges thereby giving a European dimension to the experience of teachers and students in all fields and at all levels of education; and finally, to enhance the achievement of equal opportunity for free access to all forms of education throughout the Community[16].

In spite of these programmatic commitments made in 1976, ten years later the French government stated in a blue paper that in both education proper and culture, Community efforts had not produced all the tangible results hoped for and that cooperation in these fields had remained at an embryonic stage. The Single European Act of 1986, which amended the Treaties of Rome, made no reference at all to education and culture, thus giving justification to the criticisms raised that European integration had been confined to the needs and requirements of the 'trader's Europe', and had failed to add the new dimension of a 'people's Europe' advocated by the Community itself[17]. The French Blue Paper tried to remedy this weakness by proposing a pragmatic ('à la carte') method of cooperation in education and culture, with active participants only those of the member states which were willing to be involved, thus avoiding any form of preliminary debate on the legal or institutional framework of the cooperation[18].

The French challenge for 'à la carte' cooperation in education, in the absence of a general agreement, was finally avoided by a common decision to introduce cooperation in the field of education on the basis of the 'Community method' on secondary legislation. But they did so having paid, under the force of the circumstance, a real price: it was decided by the Court of Justice ruling that any form of education which prepares for a qualification for a particular profession is vocational training, for which the Community has had jurisdiction.

The Erasmus programme, adopting for the mobility of university students, was driven by the judgement of the Court of Justice to fall exclusively within the scope of the common vocational training policy as provided for in Article 128 of the Treaty. The main objective of the programme has been to increase significantly such mobility in the Community and thus promote greater cooperation between universities, so defined as to cover all types of post-secondary education and training establishments which offer qualifications or diplomas of that level. The underlying principle was that the intellectual potential of the individual universities throughout the Community could be much more effectively exploited by providing a network for increasing student and university teacher mobility and other forms of inter-university cooperation throughout the Community.

In the realisation that cooperation in the field of education, as expressed by Community programmes such as Erasmus and Lingua, significantly enhances the value of measures taken by member states, the Community decided to establish the action programme 'Socrates' in the context of the new legal framework (Article 126) of the European Union Treaty. This programme, which complements the 'Leonardo' established to implement the European Community vocational training policy, is intended to contribute to the development of quality education and training and the creation of an open European area for cooperation in education.

The areas of action of the programme include higher education cooperation (covered by Erasmus), school education cooperation (covered now by Comenius), advancement of language skills in the Community (covered mainly by Lingua), development of open and distance education, and promotion of the exchange of information and experience (including Eurydice and Arion)[19].

The enhancement of transnational cooperation between universities, especially through the development of inter-university cooperation programmes (ICPs), aims at gradually reinforcing the European dimension in higher education[20]. In school education, especially primary and secondary education, the strengthening of the European dimension implies the creation of multilateral partnerships between schools built around a European education project (EEP), the advancement of the education of the children of migrant workers and those of the occupational travellers, and the improvement of the skills of the education teaching staff.

The promotion of language skills is a key factor in establishing an open European area for cooperation in education, thereby strengthening understanding and solidarity between the peoples of the Community, without sacrificing any of the linguistic and cultural diversity. Similarly, the development of open and distance education is a key factor enabling citizens to take advantage of an open European area for cooperation in education, thereby contributing to the quality of education[21].

In the same direction works the promotion of exchange of information and experience, on questions of common educational policy interest, and the enhancement of the European dimension in all areas of adult education (general, cultural and social), by means of transnational cooperation and exchange of experience between adult education institutions and organisations.

Exhibit 3.8: Legislative binding rules on cooperation in education

Council Decision 87/327/EEC of 15 June 1987 adopting the European Community Action Scheme for the Mobility of University Students (ERASMUS): OJ L166/20, 25. 6. 1987, as amended by **Council Decision 89/663/EEC** of 14 December 1989: OJ L395/23, 30. 12. 1989.

Council Directive 90/366/EEC of 28 June 1990 on the right of residence for students: OJ L180, 13. 7. 1990.

Council and Parliament Decision 95/819/EC of 14 March 1995 establishing the Community action programme 'Socrates': OJL87, 20. 4. 1995.

Council and Parliament Decision 95/2493/EC of 23 October 1995 establishing 1996 as the 'European year of lifelong learning': OJ L256/45, 26. 10. 1995.

3.3.7 Cooperation with associated countries in education and training

Education and vocational training cooperation has not been confined exclusively to member states. The Community has also developed co-operation links with several associated countries. Three categories of such countries could be identified here. One includes former EFTA countries and Cyprus and Malta, all of which have had a liberal democratic experience and also satisfy the Community rules for gaining full membership[22]. Another category includes the former socialist countries of central and eastern Europe (including the states of the former Soviet Union) which have recently been in a process of social and political transformation which increases the prospect for full membership. And the third category includes two states, USA and Canada, with which the Community and the member states have had historic economic, political and military ties.

In the case of the EFTA countries, with which there has been advanced economic cooperation[23], the Community decided in the early 1990s to extend to them the application of two basic education and training programmes, the Erasmus and the Comett. The objective was to strengthen and encourage cooperation between universities and industry within the European framework in regard to initial and continuing training in advanced technology. This is in response to technological change and social changes in the context of the completion of the internal market and the strengthening of its economic and social cohesion (Comett II). Also to facilitate the establishment and operation of European university networks designed to stimulate the mobility of students, through the academic recognition of diplomas and periods of study, and teaching staff, thereby increasing their mutual understanding of the training aspects of the higher education systems of the host states. More recently and for the same reasons, the Community decided to include Cyprus and Malta, under the same rules as applied to the EFTA countries, in its operations on education, training and youth within the framework of the Leonardo, Socrates and Youth for Europe programmes[24].

The cooperation in education and vocational training with the associated countries of central and eastern Europe (CCEE) has been established, following the Phare and Tacis programmes[25], through the European Training Foundation and the trans-European cooperation scheme for higher education (Tempus). The Foundation, whose seat is in Turin, aims at contributing to the development of the vocational training systems of the countries of central and eastern Europe through the enhancement of effective cooperation between the Community and those countries in the field of vocational training. The Community provides not only financial assistance but also its know-how, implying the experience gained in the area of vocational training in implementing a common policy in this field. The Foundation works in the training field, which covers initial and continuing vocational training as well as retraining for young people and adults, by providing assistance in the definition of training needs and priorities. It also acts as a clearing house to provide the Community and the countries concerned with information on current initiatives and future needs in the training field[26].

The Tempus cooperation scheme builds on the experience and expertise gained within the Community in the areas particularly of inter-university cooperation and student exchange (Erasmus) as well as of industry-university cooperation (Comett). The scheme provides support for joint European projects linking universities and/or enterprises in eligible countries with partners in the Community, and also direct financial support for student and academic staff mobility as well as for exchanges of young people and youth organisers between member states and eligible countries. The idea behind it is that cooperation of this kind tends to operate as an appropriate instrument for the transformation of their higher education systems in the context of social reforms, which include economic reform and recovery as well as democratic and administrative reforms. After all, cooperation in higher education reinforces and consolidates a large array of relations between the different peoples of Europe, promotes common cultural values, allows fruitful exchanges of ideas and facilitates multinational activities in the scientific, socio-economic and commercial spheres[27].

The cooperation programmes with the USA and Canada in higher education and training are built on the Transatlantic Declaration of 1990 which provides for the strengthening of mutual cooperation in various fields including exchanges and joint projects in education, training and youth exchanges. The objective is to promote mutual understanding, improve the quality of human resource development and of transatlantic student mobility, promote partnerships among higher education and vocational training institutions, and introduce a new dimension, both European and American, to transatlantic cooperation in higher education and vocational training[28].

Exhibit 3.9: Legislative binding rules on cooperation with associated countries in education and training

1 **Cooperation with EFTA states and Cyprus and Malta**

Council Decisions 90/190/EEC, 90/191/EEC, 90/192/EEC, 90/193/EEC, 90/194/EEC and 90/195/EEC of 29 March 1990 concerning the conclusion of six bilateral agreements between the EEC and the Republics of Austria, Finland and Iceland, the Kingdoms of Norway and Sweden, and the Swiss Confederation establishing cooperation in the field of training in the context of the implementation of Comett II (1990–1994): OJ L102/1 to 60, 21. 4. 1990.

Council Decisions 91/611/EEC, 91/612/EEC, 91/613/EEC, 91/614/EEC, 91/615/EEC, 91/616/EEC and 91/617/EEC of 28 October 1991 concerning the conclusion of seven bilateral agreements between the EEC and the Republics of Austria, Finland and Iceland, the Kingdoms of Norway and Sweden, the Swiss Confederation, and the Principality of Liechtenstein establishing cooperation in the field of education and training within the framework of the Erasmus programme: OJ L332/1 to 71, 3. 12. 1991.

Council Decisions(to be signed) of 21 December 1995 concerning the conclusion of two bilateral agreements between the EC and the Republics of Cyprus and Malta establishing cooperation in the fields of education, training and youth within the framework of the Leonardo, Socrates and Youth for Europe III programmes: OJ L.....(Bull EC 12–1995, point 1. 3. 1979).

2 **Cooperation with central and eastern European countries**

Council Regulation 90/1360/EEC of 7 May 1990 establishing a European Training Foundation: OJ L131, 23. 5. 1990, as amended by **Council Regulation 94/2063/EEC** of 27 July 1994: OJ L216, 20. 8. 1994.

Council Decision 90/233/EEC of 7 May 1990 establishing a trans-European mobility scheme for university studies (Tempus: 1990 to 1994): OJ L131, 23. 5. 1990, as amended by **Council Decision 90/240/EEC** of 28 April 1992: OJ L122, 7. 5. 1992.

Council Decision 93/246/EEC of 29 April 1993 adopting the second phase of the trans-European cooperation scheme for higher education (Tempus II:1994 to 1998): OJL112/34, 6. 5. 1993, as amended by **Council Decision 96/663/EC** of 21 November 1996: OJ L306, 28. 11. 1996.

3   **Cooperation with the USA and Canada**

Council Decision 95/487/EC of 23 October 1995 concerning the conclusion of an agreement between the EC and the USA establishing a cooperation programme in higher education and vocational education and training: OJ L279/11, 22. 11. 1995.

Council Decision 95/523/EC of 27 November 1995 concerning the conclusion of an agreement between the EC and Canada establishing a cooperation programme in higher education and training: OJ L300/18, 13. 12. 1995.

3.4   Executive Non-Binding Acts

The legally restricted Community competence on education proper and to a lesser extent on vocational training has forced the Community to express its positions in the form of non-binding acts, be they Council resolutions or Commission communications. There are two categories of these non-binding acts. One includes those non-binding acts which have already reinforced legislative binding rules in the Community in the field of education and training, as those examined above. While the other category includes non-binding acts which are currently subject to broader discussion in the member states and the Community itself. In what follows, I consider the latter category, defined mainly by the White Paper on education and training [COM(95)590], and of the former, the most important documents produced in the late 1980s and the early 1990s.

The point of departure for a serious discussion in the Community about cooperation in education and training has been the 1976 Council resolution wherein the Community action programme was outlined. This programme dealt first of all with the Community migrant workers and their children expressing the willingness of the member states to develop better facilities for the education and vocational training of those nationals coming from other member states of the Community or from non-member countries. This concern was linked with several other issues such as the promotion of closer relations between the educational systems of the member states, the circulation of information between those responsible for education and those receiving it at all levels, the teaching of foreign languages so as to offer all students the opportunity of learning at least one other Community language, the achievement of equal opportunity for free access to all forms of education, and the cooperation in the field of higher education.

The principle of giving a European dimension to education and training was also introduced, and later became the main subject of the 1988 Council resolution. The objective was to gradually incorporate the European dimension in the educational systems of the member states and thus strengthen in young people a sense of European identity and prepare them to take part in the economic and social development of the Community. It also aimed at the promotion of measures to boost contacts between students and teachers from different countries in order to give them direct experience of European integration and the realities of life in other European countries. And all these in the belief that the European dimension in education and training is an element contributing to the development of the Community and achievement of the objective of creating a unified internal market.

Thus viewed, the principle of the European dimension in education tends to define the Community actions not only in education proper but also in vocational training. In the latter, the guiding principle of the Community action has been the belief that improved training represents an essential prerequisite for dealing with economic restructuring and the social and occupational changes associated with it. In this conjuncture, 'human or intangible capital' tends to play a growing role as it includes not only professional qualifications and technological competences but also the ability to organise and develop an entrepreneurial spirit.

This is the context of the information society which tends to become, under the force of the circumstance, a 'teaching and learning' society wherein each individual builds up his or her own qualifications. Thus, Community policies for professional qualifications necessarily evolve in the framework of a double political objective: ensuring free movement of persons (human capital) and developing common policies for vocational training.

The mobility of persons within the Community, which depends on genuine recognition of knowledge verified through paper qualifications and also derived from partial skills on the basis of reliable accreditation systems, is one answer to the 'factors of upheaval' raised in the information society. The other is to build up a broad base of knowledge necessary to grasp the meaning of things, to understand and to create, and also to adjust to the economic and employment situation. This being the case, promoting the European dimension in education and training becomes, as the 1995 White Paper points out [COM(95)590], 'a necessity for efficiency in the face of internationalisation' and also the means for avoiding 'the risk of a watered-down European society'.

This vocational training challenge leaves very little space for the development of Community measures on education proper. Although the Community recognises the civilising role of higher education and the importance of its academic/scholarly stream, it nevertheless suggests that the study of the humanities nowadays can have a purpose only if associated with professional/technical education. This entails, according to the 1995 White Paper, the end of the debate on educational principles, simply because 'training for employment' and the acquisition of 'broad knowledge base' are no longer two separate or contradictory things. For, not only are bridges being built between school and the business sector, but there is also increasing recognition for the importance of general knowledge in using vocational skills[29].

This being the general framework of the Community measures (both binding and non-binding) on education and training, the question now is how one evaluates the results of the application of the Community action programmes. I propose to proceed with a double evaluation: one is **quantitative** centred on Community funding for education and training and on mobility of students and teaching staff; and the other is **qualitative** and deals with specific central issues which themselves defined the content and the form of the Community policies on education and training.

Exhibit 3.10: Executive non-binding acts on education and training

Council resolution (and of the Ministers of Education meeting within the Council) of 9 February 1976 comprising an action programme in the field of education: OJC38, 19 February 1976.

Council resolution (and of the Ministers of Education meeting within the Council) of 24 May 1988 on the European dimension in education: OJ C177, 6 July 1988.

Commission communication entitled 'Education in the European Community: Medium-term perspectives, 1989–92': COM(88)280 final, 18 May 1988.

Commission communication entitled 'Education and training in the European Community: Guidelines for the medium term, 1989–92': COM(89)236 final, 2 June 1989.

Commission memorandum on 'higher education in the European Community': COM(91)349 final, 5 November 1991.

Commission memorandum on 'vocational training in the European Community in the 1990s': COM(91)397 final, 12 December 1991.

Commission working paper entitled 'Guidelines for Community action in the field of education and training': COM(93)183 final, 5 May 1993.

Commission green paper on 'the European dimension of education': COM(93)457 final, 29 September 1993.

Commission white paper on 'Growth, competitiveness and employment: The challenges and ways forward into the 21st century': COM(93)700 final, 5 December 1993.

Commission white paper on education and training entitled 'Teaching and learning: towards the learning society': COM(95) 590 final, 29 November 1995.

Commission communication on 'learning in the information society: Action plan for a European education initiative, 1996–98': COM(96)471 final, 2 October 1996.

Commission green paper on 'Education, training, research: the obstacles to transnational mobility: COM(96)462 final, 2 October 1996.

Council conclusions of 6 May 1996 on the White Paper 'Teaching and learning: towards the learning society': OJ C195/1, 6 July 1996.

Notes

1 See Resolution of the Council and the Ministers of Education meeting within the Council of 9 February 1976, comprising an action programme in the field of education: OJ C38 19. 2. 1976. See also Council Resolution of 21 January 1974 concerning a social action programme: OJ C13, 12. 2. 1974; Resolution of Ministers of Education meeting within the Council, 6 June 1974, on cooperation in the field of education: OJ C98, 20. 8. 1974; and Council Resolution of 9 February 1976 on an action programme for migrant workers and members of their families: OJ C34, 14. 2. 1976.

2 See Parliament Resolutions (i) on the implementation of Directive 77/486/EEC on the education of the children of migrant workers: OJ C125, 11. 5. 1987, and (ii) on cultural plurality and the problems of school education for children of migrants in the European Community: OJ C42, 15. 2. 1993.

3 See also COM(83)482 final; and Council Resolution on the comparability of vocational training qualifications: Bull.EC11-1990, point 1.3.43.

4 cf. COM(94)596 final; COM(84) 446 final; Parliament Resolution on the Commission communication on recognition of qualifications for academic and professional purposes: OJ C323, 4. 12. 1995; and Council Conclusions on the synergies between aca-

demic recognition and professional recognition of qualifications in the Community, adopted on 6 May 1996, Bull. EC5-1996, point 1.3.61.

5　cf. COM(78) 222 final; COM(88) 203 final; and COM(88) 841 final.

6　cf. Council Resolution of 31 March 1995 on improving and diversifying language learning and teaching within the education systems of the European Union: OJ C207/01, 12. 8. 1995.

7　cf. COM(93) 194 final; COM(94) 280 final; and COM(95) 458 final.

8　See also COM(90) 378 final; COM(91) 355 final; SEC(92) 1262; and COM(93) 524 final.

9　See Council Resolution of 21 January 1974 concerning a social action programme: OJ C13/1, 12. 2. 1974.

10　cf. Community Charter of the Fundamental Social Rights of Workers, adopted in Strasbourg on 9 December 1989 by the member states, with the exception of the United Kingdom, cf. 'First Report on the Application of the Community Charter of the Fundamental Social Rights of Workers', Social Europe 1/92, and 'Second Report on the Application of the Community Charter of the Fundamental Social Rights of Workers', Social Europe, Supplement 1/93.

11　cf. COM(87) 705 final; COM(85) 767 final; Council Resolution of 13 December 1976 concerning measures to be taken to improve the preparation of young people to work and to facilitate their transition from education to working life: OJ C308, 30. 12. 1976.

12　cf. COM(92) 457 final; COM(93) 700 final (especially ch.7); COM(94) 528 final; Council Resolution of 2 June 1983 concerning vocational measures and new information technologies: OJ C166, 25. 6. 1983; and Council Resolution of 19 September 1983 on measures relating to the introduction of new information technology in education: OJ C256, 24. 9. 1983.

13　cf. COM(86) 780 final; COM(89) 567 final; COM(94) 418 final; Council Resolution of 5 June 1989 on continuing vocational training: OJ C148, 15. 6. 1989; European Parliament Resolution on the IRIS network and vocational training for women: OJ C 194/361, 19. 7. 1993; and Commission Recommendation 87/567/EEC of 24 November 1987 on vocational training for women: OJ L342/35, 4. 12. 1987.

14　cf. COM(91)397 final; Council Resolution of 11 June 1993 on vocational education and training in the 1990s: OJC186/2, 8. 7. 1993; Council Resolution of 5 December 1994 on the quality and attractiveness of vocational education and training: OJ C374/01, 30. 12. 1994; and Council Resolution of 24 July 1995 on the importance and implications of the quality of vocational training: OJ C207/03, 12. 8. 1995.

15　cf. Resolution of the Ministers for Education meeting within the Council of 6 June 1974 on cooperation in the field of education: OJ C98, 20. 8. 1974.

16　cf. Resolution of the Council and the Ministers for Education meeting within the Council of 9 February 1976 comprising an action programme in the field of education: OJ C38, 19. 2. 1976. See also the General Report of the Education Committee agreed to in substance by the Council of Ministers for Education meeting within the Council at their session of 27 June 1980 (Council of the EC, 1986, pp.46-69).

17　On the 'people's Europe', see Commission of the EC, "A People's Europe: Reports from the ad hoc Committee" (Adonnino Report), Bulletin of the EC, Supplement 7/85.

18　On the French Government Blue Paper, see Bull EC3 -1987, point 3.4.1.

19　Resolution of the Council and the Ministers for Education, meeting within the Council, of 6 December 1990 concerning the Eurydice Information Network in the European Community: OJ C329/08, 31. 12. 1990. The Arion scheme was introduced to arrange study visits for those responsible and those involved in education in member states, so as to facilitate exchanges of experience and information about innovations. Over 5000 education experts have already had an opportunity to study developments in education policy on the spot in the member states, reporting back to policy makers in their own countries (EC, 1994, p.38).

20 cf. Conclusions of the Council and the Ministers of Education meeting within the Council of 27 November 1992 on measures for developing the European dimension in higher education: OJ C336/03, 19. 12. 1992. See also Conclusions of the Council and of the Ministers for Education meeting within the Council of 11 June 1993 on furthering an open European space for cooperation within higher education: OJ C186/01, 8. 7. 1993.

21 cf. COM(91)388 final; and Conclusions of the Council and the Ministers of Education meeting within the Council of 1 June 1992 on the development of open and distance learning in the European Community: OJ C151/3, 16. 6. 1992. See also Council Decision of 7 June 1991 adopting a specific programme of research and technological development in the field of telematic systems in areas of general interest (1990-1994), and especially Area 4 in Annex I ('Flexible and Distance Learning-DELTA'): OJ C192, 16. 7. 1991.

22 Three countries of them, Austria, Finland and Sweden, have already acquired full membership, while Cyprus is expected to soon become one of the first new members.

23 In 1993 the Community concluded an agreement on the European Economic Area. See Decision of the Council and the Commission 94/1-3/ECSE, EC of 13 December 1993 on the conclusion of the Agreement on the European Economic Area between the European Communities, their member states and the Republics of Austria, Finland, and Iceland, the Kingdoms of Norway and Sweden, the Swiss Confederation, and the Principality of Liechtenstein: OJ L1/1, 3. 1. 1994.

24 Also, presumably to keep a balance with Cyprus, the Community is considering including Turkey among the beneficiary countries of these programmes. See Bull EC5-1996, point 1. 3. 63; COM(96) 199 final; and OJ C186/8 to 10, 26. 6. 1996.

25 See Council Regulation 89/3906/EEC of 18 December 1989 on economic aid to countries of central and eastern Europe (Phare programme): OJ L375, 23. 12. 1989, as amended by Council Regulation 93/1764/EEC of 30 June 1993: OJ L162, 3. 7. 1993; and Council Regulation 93/2053/EEC, Euratom of 19 July 1993 concerning the provision of technical assistance to economic reform and recovery in the independent states of the former Soviet Union and Mongolia (Tacis programme): OJ L187, 29. 7. 1993.

26 cf. COM(95)388 final.

27 cf. COM(95)344 final.

28 cf. COM(95)77 final; and COM(95)120 final.

29 The Council moderates a little this market-oriented view of the Commission by stating that 'the framework for analyzing education and training problems in Europe now and in the future should place suitable emphasis on the cultural and educational aspects as well as the strictly economic aspects of social development' (Council Conclusions of 6 May 1996 on the White Paper 'Teaching and Learning: towards the learning society': OJ C195/1, 6 July 1996).

4 The Quantitative Analysis: EU Funding and Mobility in Education and Training

The EU funding of education and training, being part of the overall Community expenditure, is analysed in the context of (i) the Community finances and with particular reference to (ii) the expenditure on vocational training through the Structural Funds (the Social Fund in particular), and (iii) the expenditure on education and training through the various education programmes. The mobility of pupils/students and teachers/academic staff is part of this latter operation.

4.1 The EU Finances

The finances are crystallised each year in the Community annual budget which includes two interrelated components: the revenue and the expenditure. In order to appreciate the magnitude of the Community expenditure on education and training, it is necessary to briefly present a general picture of the overall finances in terms of both revenue and expenditure. The period under consideration in this study is the last decade, i.e. from 1987 to 1996.

In this period the revenue of the Community has increased in absolute terms from 3.6 billion ECU in 1987 to approximately 8.2 billion ECU in 1996. This increase was reinforced by the progression of economic integration, with the establishment of the internal market and the agreement on economic and monetary union, and has mainly aimed at fostering economic and social cohesion. The individual contribution of the member states to the Community revenue depends on the level of each country's economic performance and socio-economic development. These characteristics are expressed in market terms (agricultural levies, customs duties, value added tax) and in terms of gross national wealth (GNP).

It is not surprising, therefore, that countries with relatively high GNP and large commercial activity turn out making the largest contribution to the Community's revenue. On average, Germany has contributed 28.8 per cent of the total, as compared with 19.2 per cent for France, 14.2 per cent for Italy, 12.6 per cent for the UK, 7.7 per cent for Spain, 6.3 per cent for the Netherlands, 4.1 per cent for Belgium, 2.0 per cent for Denmark, 1.4 per cent for Greece, 1.3 per cent for Portugal, 0.9 per cent for Ireland and 0.2 per cent for Luxembourg (Figure 4.1).

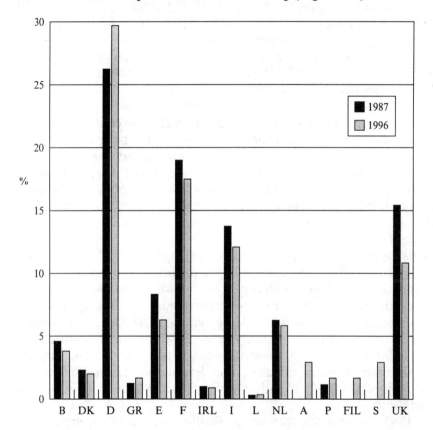

Figure 4.1 Community revenue (%) by member state, 1987, 1996
Source: Appendix, Table 1

Germany's gross domestic product (GDP) in 1993, for instance, was 29.5 per cent of total EUR12, as compared with 19.4 per cent for France, 15.3 per cent for Italy, 14.6 per cent for the UK, 7.4 per cent for Spain, 4.9 per cent for the Netherlands, 3.3 per cent for Belgium, 2.1 per cent for Denmark, 1.4 per cent for Greece, 1.3 per cent for Portugal, 0.7 per cent for Ireland and 0.2 per cent for Luxembourg (EC,1995, table 2.1).

Likewise, Germany's total exports (value) in 1993 were 67.3 per cent of total EUR12, as compared with 38.3 per cent for France, 31.8 per cent for the UK, 29.8 per cent for Italy, 24.6 per cent for the Netherlands, 22.0 per cent for Belgium/Luxembourg, 11.3 per cent for Spain, 6.5 per cent for Denmark, 5.0 per cent for Ireland, 2.7 per cent for Portugal, and 1.5 per cent for Greece. If compared on a world basis, Germany's total exports (value) represented in 1993, for instance, 8.9 per cent of total world exports, as compared with 13.2 per cent for EUR12, 12.5 per cent for EEA (European Economic Area) countries, 10.9 per cent for the USA, 8.5 per cent for Japan, 5.1 per cent for France, 4.2 per cent for the UK, 4.0 per cent for Italy, and smaller percentages for the other EU countries (EC,1995, Table 6.3).

In a balanced budget, as is generally the case in the EU, the Community revenue gives a clear indication of its overall expenditure. The interesting point is that the level of the Community expenditure is far below that of the expenditure of the member states. In the period under consideration, for example, the average annual total Community expenditure represented only 2.2 per cent of the corresponding total public expenditure in the member states. In the same period, the Community expenditure represented only 1.06 per cent of the Community GDP (Figure 4.2).

This suggests that the process of European integration has been more a process of market integration, wherein the forces of the market define the economic outcome, than a process of real economic integration, wherein the economic performance is conditioned not only by the forces of the market but also by political intervention in the function of wealth redistribution at the Community level. In the context of this neo-liberal, market-oriented, approach to integration, it comes as no surprise that the gap between advanced and less developed member states (and regions) has only slightly narrowed in the history of European integration.

In 1985, for instance, the average GDP per capita of the three more advanced member states (Denmark, Germany, France, excluding Luxembourg) was 14 per cent higher than the average Community GDP (EUR15=100), while that of the three less developed member states (Greece, Ireland, Portugal) was 43 per cent lower than the EUR15 average. In the ten-year period afterwards, the average annual GDP per capita of the said advanced member states has been found at 11 per cent above the average Community GDP, while that of the aforementioned less developed member states has still remained below the Community average at 35.6 per cent (Appendix, Table 18).

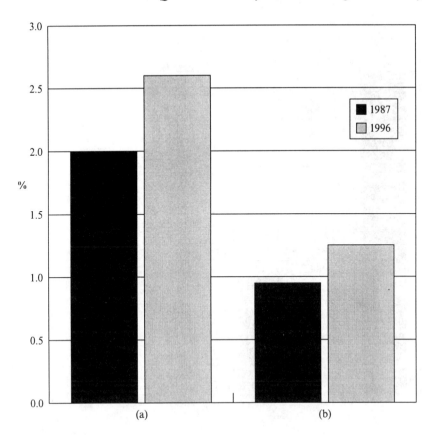

Figure 4.2 Community expenditure (a) as % of public expenditure in member states and (b) as % of Community GDP, 1987, 1996
Source: Appendix, Table 2

This situation is congruent with the actual distribution of Community expenditure. In the period under consideration (1987–1996) the average annual amount allocated to the Structural Funds, themselves designed to foster economic and social cohesion, was just 24.3 per cent of the corresponding total Community expenditure. In the same period the amount allocated to the Social Fund (ESF), itself established to deal with unemployment and vocational training, was only 6.9 per cent of the Community total expenditure, as compared with an average annual of 3.4 per cent for research and technological development, and 0.34 per cent for education, vocational training and youth exchanges (Figure 4.3).

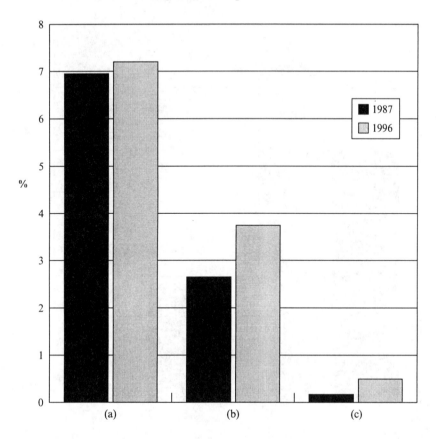

Figure 4.3 Community expenditure (%) on (a) the ESF, (b) research and technological development, and (c) education, vocational training and youth, 1987, 1996
Source: Appendix, Table 2

The preceding comparisons clearly indicate the Community priorities as regards the distribution of resources. Specifically, not only 'education and training' remains a minor issue in the actions of the Community, but also within the combined policy area called 'education and training', it is vocational training which tends to define the relevant actions of the Community. This economically-oriented approach to education and training will become apparent in the process of this analysis.

4.2 Vocational Training through the Structural Funds

The Structural Funds of the Community (European Agricultural Guidance and Guarantee Fund, Guidance Section; European Regional Development Fund; European Social Fund) are aimed at strengthening its economic and social cohesion, combating long-term unemployment and improving the skills of the labour market. Although almost all the Funds include a vocational training component in their actions, it is the Social Fund (ESF) which concentrates on human resources by providing support throughout the Community for vocational training measures and aids for employment and for the creation of self-employed activities, in order to combat long-term unemployment and integrate young people into working life[1]. For the purpose of this analysis, I concentrate on the ESF assuming that all of its actions relate, directly or indirectly, to vocational training objectives. This is a reasonable way of making-up for the missing vocational training component of the other Structural Funds.

In the period up to 1988, the ESF had been operating not only under comparatively limited resources but also without specific objectives, other than those specified in the EC Treaties, namely to render the employment of workers easier and increase their geographical and occupational mobility within the Community. The changes introduced in 1988, in view of the first Community Support Framework (CSF-I: 1989–1993), outlined five priority objectives: **Objective 1,** for promoting the development and structural adjustment of the regions whose development is lagging behind; **Objective 2,** for converting the regions, frontier regions or parts of regions seriously affected by industrial decline; **Objective 3,** for combating long-term unemployment; **Objective 4,** for facilitating the occupational integration of young people; **Objective 5(a),** for speeding up the adjustment of agricultural structures; and **Objective 5(b),** for promoting the development of rural areas[2].

The ESF operates in all objectives, with the exception of Objective 5(a), and grants assistance as follows: (i) as regards Objective 1, for vocational training whether under national secondary vocational education systems, following compulsory full-time schooling, or under apprenticeship training given outside the firm; (ii) as regards Objectives 1, 2 and 5(b), for encouraging job stability and developing new employment possibilities for the unemployed or those threatened with unemployment, particularly within the context of economic and social restructuring, and also facilitating vocational training for any working person involved in the operation of integrated programmes; and (iii) as regards its priorities

Objectives (3 and 4), for combating long-term unemployment by means of the occupational integration of persons aged over 25 who have been unemployed for more than a year, and also facilitating the occupational integration of persons under 25 from the age at which compulsory full-time schooling ends[3].

In the first two years (1989–1990) of the operation of the CSF-I, the entire amount of the ESF (6.65 per cent on the average of the Community total) was allocated to the Objective 1, while in the following three years (1991–1993) the allocation covered all five objectives. Specifically, on the average, 48.4 per cent for Objective 1, 8.1 per cent for Objective 2, 35.9 per cent for Objectives 3 and 4, and 1.9 per cent for Objective 5(b) (Figure 4.4).

The preceding allocation of funds indicates that the central priority of the Community in this period was the fostering of initial education and training (Objective 1), and to a lesser extent the enhancement of continuing vocational training (Objectives 3 and 4). This distribution reflects the pressing needs of the social conjuncture wherein not only unemployment in general but particularly youth unemployment was at high levels. In 1991, for instance, the rate of unemployment in the EUR12 was 8.8 per cent (about 13.7 million people), of which 33.4 per cent represented unemployment of young people aged under 25 (EC, 1995, Tables 3.21 and 3.22).

The same concern appears during the operation of the second Community Support Framework (CSF-II:1994–1999). In view of the introduction of CSF-II, the Community made some changes in the priority objectives of the Structural Funds in order to take into consideration the needs raised by the social and economic changes in the era of the new technologies. Specifically, Objectives 3 and 4 were combined under Objective 3 aiming to combat long-term unemployment and facilitate the integration into working life of young people and persons exposed to exclusion from the labour market, while the new Objective 4 aims at facilitating the adaptation of workers of either sex to industrial changes and to changes in production systems[4].

These changes reinforced modifications on the provisions of the ESF in order for the actions taken by the Fund under the different objectives to form a coherent approach so as to improve the workings of the labour market and to develop human resources. In this new context, operations under Objective 1 are intended to (i) 'strengthen and improve education and training systems', especially through 'the training of teachers and instructors of either sex and administrative staff, by encouraging links between training centres or higher education establishments and enterprises', and also by 'financing training within the national secondary or equivalent and higher education systems which has a clear link with the labour market, new technology or economic development', and (ii) contribute to development through the training of public officials where this is necessary for 'the implementation of development and structural adjustment policies'.

Furthermore, operations under Objectives 1, 2 and 5(b) are intended (i) to 'support employment growth and stability', particularly through 'continuing training and through guidance and counselling for workers of either sex', as well as through 'support for the development of appropriate training systems, including training of instructors', and (ii) to 'boost human potential in research, science and technology', especially through 'postgraduate training and the training of managers and technicians of either sex at research establishments'.

In Objective 3 (which now combines the previous 3 and 4) operations are intended to (i) 'facilitate the occupational integration of unemployed persons exposed to long-term unemployment', particularly through 'vocational training and pre-training', including 'upgrading of basic skills, guidance and counselling', and (ii) 'facilitate the occupational integration of young people in search of employment' through operations as described above, including the possibility 'of up to two years' or more initial 'vocational training leading to a vocational qualification', and also the possibility 'of vocational training equivalent to compulsory schooling', provided that 'by the end of that training the young people are old enough to join the labour market'.

Finally in the new Objective 4, operations are intended to facilitate the 'adaptation of workers of either sex', especially those threatened with unemployment, 'to industrial change and to changes in production systems', in particular through (i) the 'anticipation of labour market trends and vocational qualification requirements', (ii) 'vocational training and retraining, guidance and counselling', and (iii) 'assistance for the improvement and development of appropriate training systems'[5].

Thus, the re-oriented Social Fund now has the main objective to foster not only initial vocational training and continuing training, but also advanced training (Objectives 1 and 4) in cooperation with the higher-education institutions of the member states. In this last capacity, the Social Fund complements Community operations in education and training pursued, as indicated below, through the Community education programmes. In the first three years (1994–1996) of the operation of the CSF-II, Objective 1 actions received on average 52.5 per cent of total Social Fund expenditure, as compared with 31.1 per cent for Objective 3,

8.7 per cent for Objective 2, 4.1 per cent for Objective 4, and 2.5 per cent for Objective 5(b) (Figure 4.4).

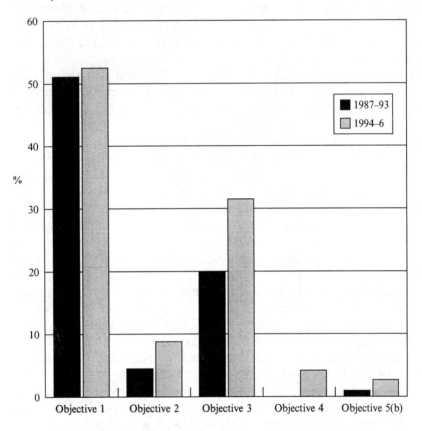

Figure 4.4 ESF financing (%) by Objective, 1987–1996
Source: Appendix, Table 3

The distribution of the funds by member state gives a further indication of the priorities of the Community and the special needs of the individual states. In the period of the first Community support framework (CSF-I: 1989–1993), of the total amount allocated for Objective 1, the less developed Mediterranean countries and Ireland got the greater proportion: 21.4 per cent for Spain, 19.6 per cent for Portugal, 16.6 per cent for Greece, 14.6 per cent for Ireland and 13.8 per cent for Italy, as compared with 7.9 per cent for Germany (due to payments to New Lander), 3.1 per cent for France and 2.9 per cent for the UK. It should be mentioned here that three of the less developed member states (Greece,

Portugal, Ireland, whose per capita GDP, on the basis of the figures for the last three years, is less than 75 per cent of the Community average) fall entirely under the provisions of Objective 1 and thus get support only from this Objective.

In Objective 2 actions, three countries receive the greater proportion: 40.0 per cent for the UK, 17.4 per cent for Spain and 16.6 per cent for France. Likewise, in Objectives 3 and 4, the UK gets 27.8 per cent, France 22.9 per cent, Germany 13.5 per cent, Italy 12.3 per cent and Spain 11.8 per cent. Finally, in Objective 5(b) France receives the highest proportion (39.5 per cent), followed by the UK (15.2 per cent), Germany (14.9 per cent), Spain (10.5 per cent) and Italy (10.2 per cent).

In the period of the second Community Support Framework (CSF-II: 1994–1999), the pattern of the distribution seems to follow similar lines. In 1994, for instance, the less developed countries plus Germany dominate in Objective 1 actions: 21.1 per cent for Spain, 19.8 per cent for Greece, 16.7 per cent for Germany (again due to New Lander), 15.1 per cent for Ireland, 12.1 per cent for Portugal and 7.9 per cent for Italy.

In Objective 2 actions, four countries are at the top: the UK with 36.4 per cent of the total, France with 18.4 per cent, Germany with 15.3 per cent and Italy with 12.0 per cent. Likewise, in Objective 3 the UK gets 31.8 per cent of the total, followed by France (20.3 per cent), Germany (11.5 per cent), the Netherlands (10.1 per cent), Italy (9.5 per cent) and Spain (9.3 per cent). In the new Objective 4, three countries are the greater beneficiaries: France with 35.4 per cent, Italy with 22.5 per cent and Spain with 20.6 per cent. While in Objective 5(b), France gets the higher proportion (48 per cent), followed by Germany (19 per cent) and Italy (13 per cent).

In the entire period examined here (1989–1994) and for all the Objectives, eight countries get the highest proportion of the total amount allocated. These are, Spain with 17.2 per cent, the UK with 15.4 per cent, Italy with 12.1 per cent, France with 11.8 per cent, Germany with 11 per cent, Portugal with 9.9 per cent, Greece with 9.3 per cent and Ireland with 7.9 per cent (Figure 4.5).

In plain words, what these statistics suggest is that the Community priorities through the allocations of the Social Fund concentrate on three key objectives: initial vocational training, continuing vocational training, and advanced training, all three as a means of facilitating the adaptation of young people and workers to industrial changes and changes in production systems. These priorities are also the concern of the education programmes of the Community.

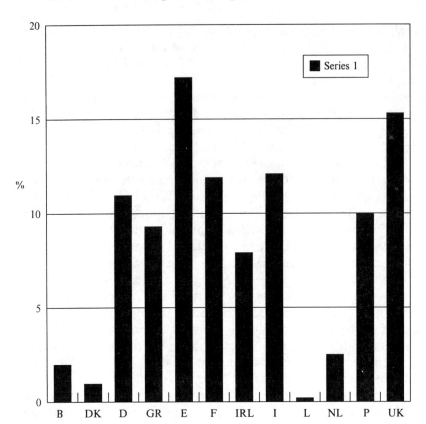

Figure 4.5 ESF financing (%) by member state, 1989–1994
Source: Appendix, Table 4

4.3   Education and Training through the Education Programmes

There are here three interrelated areas in which Community action takes place: education proper, vocational training, and youth exchanges. In the period under consideration (1987–1996), of the total Community expenditure on education, vocational training and youth through the education programmes, 49.9 per cent of the average was allocated to education, 42.6 per cent to vocational training, and 7.5 per cent to youth exchanges (Figure 4.6).

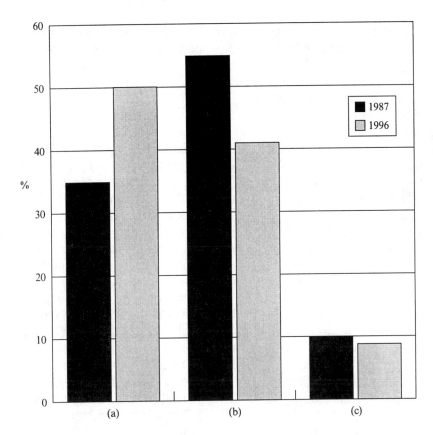

Figure 4.6 Community financing (%) on (a) education, (b) vocational training, and (c) youth, 1987, 1996
Source: Appendix, Table 5

This distribution of funds may be a little misleading if one considers the fact that programmes cited on education proper (e.g. Socrates, Erasmus, Lingua) have a very strong vocational training component. This means that the actual allocations on vocational training are much higher constituting in fact the key priority of the Community actions. Overall, however, the Community spending on education and training is not so significant as the figures may suggest, if this expenditure is compared with expenditure in similar Community actions. In 1987, for instance, the Community expenditure on education, vocational training and youth was 56.34 million ECU, of which MECU 19.71 was allocated to education, as here defined (Appendix, Table 5), MECU 30.87 to vocational training and MECU 5.76 to youth. In the same year the Community spent a total of 52.8 million ECU for the European Schools alone, established mainly to receive the children of the Community employees (EC Budget 1987, p.356). This elitist approach, which is found in every year of Community spending, characterises almost all the Community education and training programmes.

The distribution of Community expenditure by education and training programme is a clear indication of the Community priorities. Of the total Community expenditure allocated through the education programmes in the period 1987–1996, 27.1 per cent on the average was for Erasmus, 16.3 per cent for Comett, 15.6 per cent for Socrates, 12.8 per cent for Leonardo, 8.5 per cent for Lingua, 8.5 per cent for Petra, 5.8 per cent for Youth for Europe, 4.5 per cent for Force, 0.5 per cent for Eurydice/Arion and 0.4 per cent for Eurotecnet (Figure 4.7).

The ten education and training programmes mentioned above can be placed into three groups: (a) for education proper, which includes Socrates, Erasmus, Lingua and Eurydice/Arion[6], there is an allocation of 51.7 per cent of the total; (b) for vocational training, which includes Leonardo, Comett, Petra, Force and Eurtecnet, there is an allocation of 43.8 per cent of the total; and (c) for youth, which includes the Youth for Europe programme, there is an allocation of 4.5 per cent of the total. These three categories are now analysed in turn[7].

(A) Education: The **Erasmus** has mainly been based on inter-university cooperation programmes (ICPs). The institutions involved, based on one or more approved Erasmus ICPs, have increased from 526 in the academic year 1988/89 to 1707 in the academic year 1994/95. In the total 1707, France had the largest involvement (411 institutions), followed by the UK (220 institutions), Germany (217 institutions) and Belgium (142 institutions) [Appendix, Table 7(a)]. This is indicative of the fact that three languages – French, English, German – dominate in the programme, as in the overall activities of the Community.

Of the total Community funds committed to the programme, the greatest proportion (69 per cent on average) was for student grants (Action 2), as compared with an average of 23.6 per cent for ICPs and study visits (Action 1), 5.2 per cent for publications, evaluation and monitoring (Action 4), and 2.2 per cent for institutional and network grants (Action3) (Figure 4.8).

The allocation of student grants per member state follows the pattern of the distribution of institutions mentioned above, with the addition of Italy and Spain to prominent positions. Specifically, of the total amount allocated to student grants (Action 2), Germany gets 17.6 per cent on

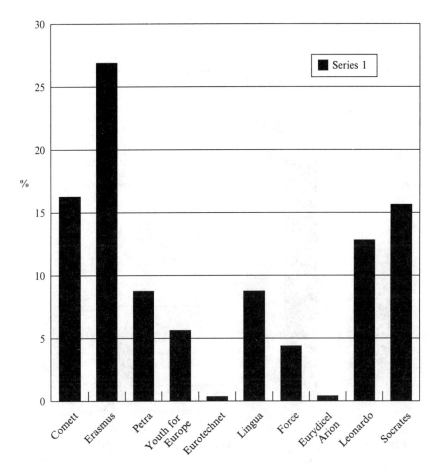

Figure 4.7 Community funding (%) by education and training programme, 1987–1996
Source: Appendix, Table 6

average, as compared with 14 per cent for France, 13.9 per cent for Italy, 13.2 per cent for the UK and 11.1 per cent for Spain (Figure 4.9).

The main reason for the relatively low proportion the UK gets in the allocation of student grants, as compared with the high proportion of institutions involvement in the Erasmus ICPs, is that the UK operates mostly as a host country for students. This means that the UK receives a higher proportion of Erasmus students than it sends abroad to other member states. Specifically, of the total planned student mobility in the Erasmus programme, the ratio between sent/received students was 1:1.2 for the UK, as compared for instance with 1:1.03 for France, 1: 0.97 for

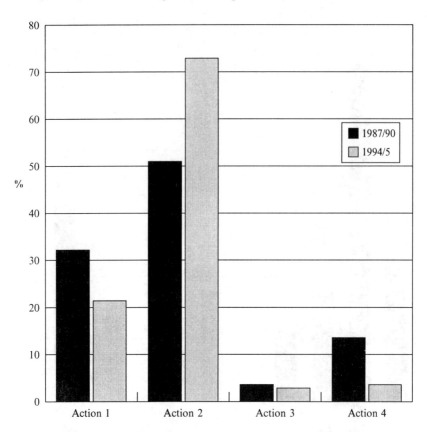

Figure 4.8 Erasmus funding (%) by Action, 1989/90, 1994/95
Source: Appendix, Table 7(b)

Spain, 1:0.94 for Germany, 1:0.88 for Italy, and 1:0.82 for Greece [Appendix, Table 7(d)].

In absolute terms the annual student mobility represents a very small fraction of the total student population in the Community. In 1992/93, for instance, of a total 8.47 million[8] higher education students in the EU (12 countries), only 80100 students entered the Erasmus planned student mobility programme, which was less than 1 per cent of the total. This is indeed an elitist characteristic of the programme[9].

The picture is somehow similar in the **Lingua** programme as well. First of all, of the total amount allocated to the programme, the action on joint education projects (Action IV) received the relatively largest proportion (25.6 per cent), as compared with 23.1 per cent for Action I (:in-service training of language teachers), 19.5 per cent for Action II

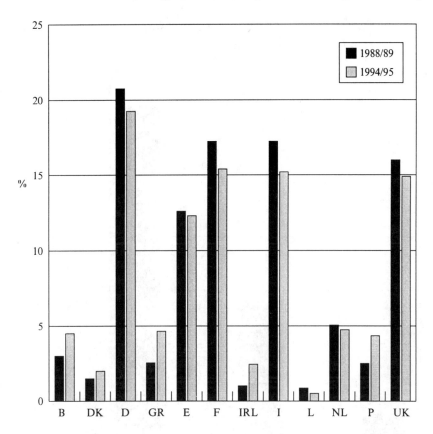

Figure 4.9 Erasmus student grants (Action 2) by country, 1988/89, 1994/95 (in %)
Source: Appendix, Table 7(c)

(:mobility of students and teachers in higher education-ICPs), 19.2 per cent for Action III (:promoting language learning in the economic world), 8.2 per cent for Action VB (: promoting learning of the least widely used, least taught languages of the Community), and 4.4 per cent for Action VA (:grants for associations, seminars and publications) [Appendix, Table 8(a)].

The mobility of participants (students and teachers) in decentralised actions (Action IA and Action IV) and in 'Higher Education' action (Action II) increased in absolute numbers from 6748 in 1990/91 to 48,805 in 1993/94. Of the total number (1990–1994), 67.3 per cent was in Action IV (:mobility of young people between the age of 16 and 25 in joint education projects), 17.6 per cent in Action II (:mobility of students in higher education), and 15.1 per cent in Action IA (:mobility of language teachers for in-service training) (Figure 4.10).

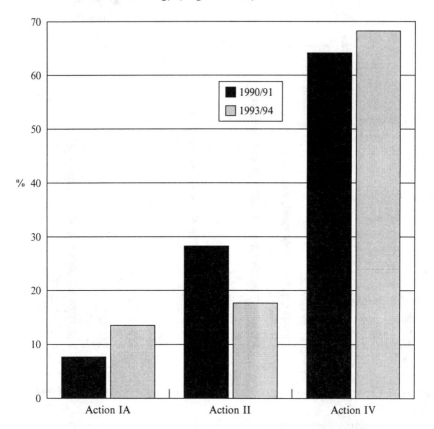

Figure 4.10 Lingua mobility of participants in Actions IA, II and IV, 1990/91, 1993/94 (in %)
Source: Appendix, Table 8(b)

The great proportion of these language teachers (Action IA) chose the UK for in-service training (44.5 per cent on average), as compared with 24.2 per cent for France, 10.1 per cent for Spain, 8.5 per cent for Germany, 4.5 per cent for Italy and smaller percentages for the other countries [Appendix, Table 8(c)]. This comes as no surprise if one takes into account the fact that the most taught foreign language in primary and secondary schools in the Community is English, followed by French. According to estimates, among primary pupils learning English, the highest percentages were found in Finland (60 per cent), Sweden (49 per cent),

Austria (48 per cent), Greece (41 per cent) and Denmark (35 per cent). In three other member states (Spain, Portugal, the Netherlands), the percentages of pupils learning English was above the European average, but to a lesser extent. In general secondary education in the Community, 88 per cent of pupils in 1992/93 were learning English. Other foreign languages were less frequently chosen: French 32 per cent, German 19 per cent and Spanish only 9 per cent[10].

In the mobility of young people and teachers accompanying them (Action IV), the largest proportion has again chosen Britain. Of the total, which increased in absolute terms from 5150 in 1990/91 to 33156 in 1993/94, 33 per cent went to the UK, as compared with 21.4 per cent for France, 9.4 per cent for Germany, 8.7 per cent for Italy, 7.5 per cent for Spain, 5.9 per cent for Denmark and smaller percentages for the other countries [Appendix, Table 8(d)].

In the centralised actions of the programme (Action IB, Action III, Action VA, Action VB), the projects accepted and the partners in the accepted projects increased by 40.9 per cent and 28.3 per cent respectively from 1991 to 1994. Of the total, 19 per cent of the projects were in Action VB (promotion of least taught languages), 16 per cent in Action IB (in-service training of language teachers), 13.6 per cent in Action VA (seminars, publications etc.) and 51.4 per cent in Action III (promotion of language learning in the economic world). This last action demonstrates the magnitude of the vocational training component in the Lingua programme. As for the partners in the accepted projects, of the total, 54.9 per cent were in Action III, 17.8 per cent in Action VB, 14.7 per cent in Action IB and 12.6 per cent in Action VA (Figure 4.11). The distribution of the projects by member state is indicative of the relative dominance of the member states with the widely used languages. Of the total projects accepted in centralised actions (1992–1994), 17.2 per cent were in the UK, 16.4 per cent in France, 12.4 per cent in Germany, 10.6 per cent in Italy, and smaller percentages in the other member states [Appendix, Table 8(f)].

In the **Tempus** (Phare) programme, four of the participating central and eastern European countries indicate the largest involvement. In the allocation of Community Funds (1990–95), Poland gets 31.3 per cent of the total, Hungary 17.7 per cent, Czechoslovakia (Czech and Slovak Republics) 14.6 per cent (of which, 59.5 per cent the Czech Republic and 40.5 per cent the Slovak Republic), and Romania 13.8 per cent. Of the rest, Bulgaria gets 10.5 per cent, Slovenia 2.2 per cent, Lithuania 2.1 per cent, Albania 2.1 per cent, Latvia 2.0 per cent, Former Yugoslavia 1.9 per cent and Estonia 1.6 per cent (Figure 4.12).

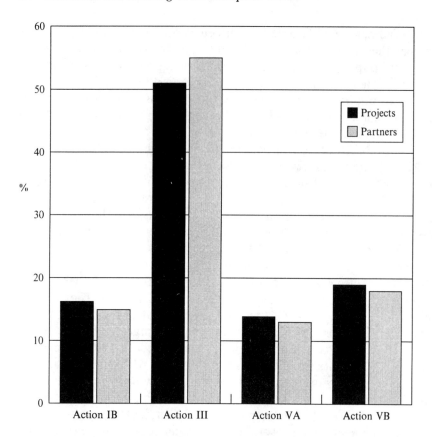

Figure 4.11 Lingua projects and partners in centralised actions, 1991–1994 (in %)
Source: Appendix, Table 8(e)

In the period 1990–1995 the programme supported a total of 2046 projects, of which 1218 were new joint European projects, 121 were joint European networks, 444 were projects in youth activities, and the remaining 263 were complementary measures [Appendix, Table 9(c)]. Again four of the participating central and eastern European countries had the greatest involvement: Poland with 26 per cent of the total, Czechoslavakia with 21.2 per cent (of which, 60.7 per cent for the Czech Republic and 39.3 per cent for the Slovak Republic), Hungary with 18.2 per cent, and Romania with 9.9 per cent of the total. The rest of the countries had weaker participation: Bulgaria with 9.1 per cent, former Yugoslavia with 4.5 per cent, Slovania with 3.6 per cent, Estonia with

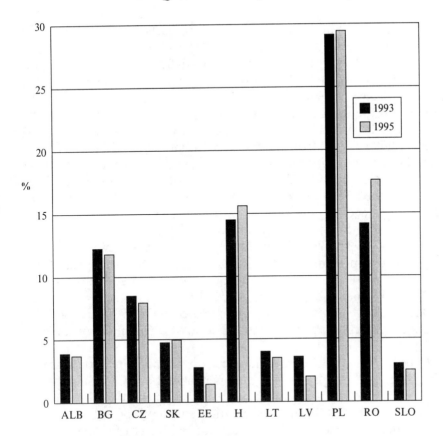

Figure 4.12 Tempus (Phare) funding (%) by country, 1993, 1995
Source: Appendix, Table 9(b)

2.2 per cent, Lithuania with 2.0 per cent, Latvia with 1.8 per cent and Albania with 1.3 per cent of the total (Appendix, Table 9(d)].

The point which needs mentioning here is that the Tempus (Phare) programme encompasses a very strong vocational training component. Specifically, of the total joint European projects approved (1992–1995), 52.7 per cent were in the area of applied sciences and technologies, as compared with 17 per cent in management and business, 11.9 per cent in social sciences and humanities, 6.8 per cent in languages and education, 6.1 per cent in natural sciences and mathematics, and the remaining 5.5 per cent in other subject areas [Appendix, Table 9(e)].

The mobility flows within the Tempus (Phare) programme represent a clear indication of the strong orientation of the eastern and central European countries towards the European Union. Specifically, the mobility flows within the joint European projects (new and renewed) include both staff and student mobility. Of the total staff mobility (51632 from 1990 to 1995), 58.16 per cent moved from CEE (Central and Eastern Europe) to the EU, 41.31 per cent from the EU to CEE and the remaining 0.53 per cent represented mobility within CEE countries. Similarly, of the total student mobility within joint European projects (27343 from 1990 to 1995), 85.42 per cent were directed from CEE to the EU, 14.39 per cent from the EU to CEE and only 0.19 per cent represented movement within CEE countries. On the whole, 60.96 per cent of total staff mobility and 85.92 per cent of total student mobility occurred in the direction from CEE to the EU countries. (Figure 4.13). The same tendencies occur in the Tempus (Tacis) programme, which is directly towards the new independent states of the former Soviet Union. In the period 1993–1995, for instance, the total Community funding amounted to approximately MECU48, of which the large proportion went to four countries: 61.5 per cent for the Russian Federation, 16 per cent for Ukraine, 8.2 per cent for Belarus, and 4.9 per cent for Kazakhstan. In the same period, approximately 5400 academic staff and 250 university students participated in a total of 296 joint European projects [Appendix, Table 9/1(a,b)].

This educational cooperation has recently found expression in some CEE countries through the Jean Monner project as well, which began in 1990 with the objective of fostering the development of European integration in universities through the creation and development of courses. In the academic year 1996/1997, two central and eastern European countries – Hungary and Poland – took part for the first time in Jean Monnet academic initiatives. Of a total of 71 such initiatives, 27 represented the introduction of permanent courses, 7 the establishment of Jean Monnet Chairs, 7 the creation of European modules, 23 the acquisition of teaching materials, and the remaining 7 represented research projects (2), doctoral grants (2) and complementary measures [Appendix, Table 19(b)].

In the EU member states, the academic initiatives of the Jean Monnet project, for the 1990–1996 period, have reached a total number of 1310 cases, of which 307 are Jean Monnet chairs, 519 permanent courses, 379 European modules, 69 research projects, and the remaining 36 represent complementary initiatives. The subject of EC law has a dominant position with 422 cases, followed by EC economics (363 cases), political sciences (260 cases), multidisciplinary initiatives (154 cases), and history initiatives (111 cases). In all these academic initiatives, five member states have a dominant position: 236 cases for the UK, 233 cases

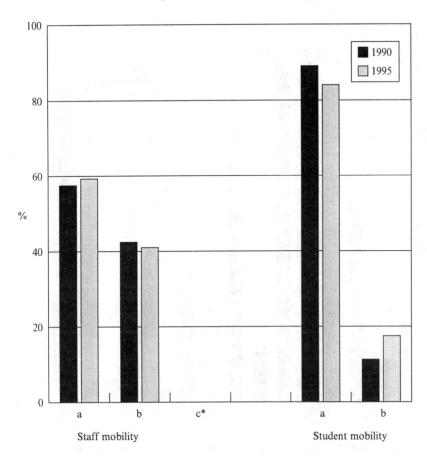

* Statistically insignificant

Figure 4.13 Tempus (Phare) mobility flows (a) from CEE to EU, (b) from EU to CEE and (c) from CEE to CEE, 1990, 1995 (in %)
Source: Appendix, Table 9(f)

for France, 193 cases for Italy, 141 cases for Germany, and 139 cases for Spain (Figure 4.14)[11].

(B) Vocational Training: In the area of **initial** vocational training to begin with the Community has made a relatively modest intervention through the **Petra** programme. In fact, of the programme's total financial support (1988–94), 35.4 per cent was allocated for Action I (:transnational training and work experience placements), as compared with 41.1 per cent for Action II [:ENTP (European Network of Training Partnerships) and YIPs (Youth Initiative Projects)], 4.0 per cent for

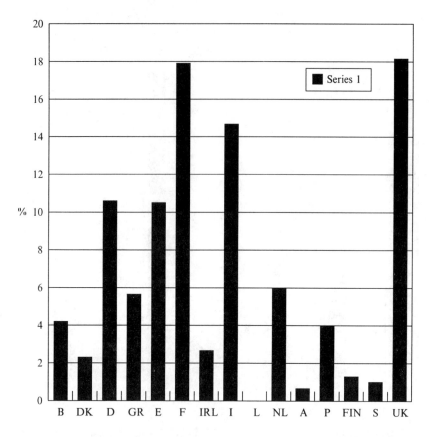

Figure 4.14 Jean Monnet academic initiatives (%) by member state, 1990–1996
Source: Appendix, Table 19(a)

Action III (:cooperation in the field of vocational guidance) and 19.5 per cent for complementary measures [Appendix, Table 10(a)].

In the period under consideration here (1988–1994) a total of 1618 projects were established in both areas of Action II: 818 in the Network (ENTP) and 800 in the youth initiatives (YIPs). The total staff (teachers, trainers, tutors) involved amounted to approximately 30000 persons, while of the young people involved in the projects (approximately 200000), 80 per cent were in Action II (ENTP and VIPs) and 20 per cent in transnational training and work experience placements [Appendix, Table 10(b)].

If placed in proper context one realises that the magnitude of the young people involvement in the projects is not very significant indeed.

In 1988, for instance, the total number of 15–19 year-olds was 26.1 million in the Community (of which, more than 10 million were in vocational upper secondary education)[12], while the Petra programme affected in the period 1988–1994 only 200000 young people, which is about 0.76 per cent of the total. It is, however, believed that the programme does contribute in a small way to the concepts of mobility and European integration by introducing a Community dimension in the area of initial vocational training[13].

In the area of **advanced** vocational training, the **Comett** programme is supposed to play the key role. In the period 1987–1989 (Comett-I) the total Community funding was MECU52.5, of which 31.8 per cent was joint continuing training projects (Strand C), 22.35 per cent for transnational student placements in enterprises (Strand Ba-BaP), 17.2 per cent for university-enterprises training partnerships (Strand A), 14.4 per cent for multimedia training initiatives (Strand D), and 2.9 per cent for transnational fellowships [Appendix, Table 11(a)]. Of the total projects accepted in the same period (Comett-I), 26.7 per cent represented French participation, as compared with 15.3 per cent for the UK, 9.4 per cent for Germany, 9.1 per cent for Spain, 7.4 per cent for Italy, and smaller percentages for the other member states [Appendix, Table 11(c)].

In the period 1990–1994 (Comett-II) the total amount allocated was MECU 221.87, of which 90.2 per cent was directed to EU member states and the remaining 9.8 per cent to the participating EFTA states. In the EU, three member states (France, Germany, UK) are together the large beneficiaries. Of the total EU, France gets on the average 17.3 per cent, the UK 17.1 per cent and Germany 14.5 per cent. Of the rest, in a good place are Italy (10.6 per cent) and Spain (8.9 per cent), followed by Greece (7.0 per cent), the Netherlands (6.3 per cent), Ireland (4.8 per cent), Belgium (4.7 per cent), Portugal (4.6 per cent), Denmark (3.3 per cent) and Luxembourg (0.9 per cent) (Figure 4.15).

The distribution of the Community allocations by Strand is indicative of the priorities involved. Of the total Comett-II amount, 35.8 per cent was allocated to transnational student placements in enterprises (Strand Ba) through 918 projects, 26.5 per cent to 304 joint training projects (Strand Cb), 13.2 per cent to 207 university-enterprises training partnerships (Strand A), 12.1 per cent to 774 advanced short courses (Strand Ca), 6.6 per cent to 30 training projects with emphasis on structural impact (Strand Cc), and 2.6 per cent to exchanges of staff between higher education and industry (Strand Bc) through 365 projects [Appendix, Table 11(e,g)].

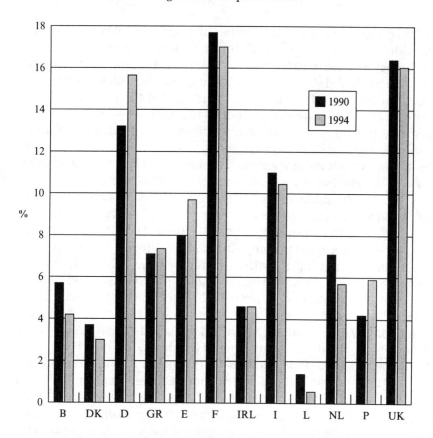

Figure 4.15 Comett-II funding (%) by member state, 1990, 1994
Source: Appendix, Table 11(d)

The preceding distributions are indicative of the mobility flows in the Comett-II programme as regards both students and fellows. Of the total (31655) transnational student placements in enterprises (Strand Ba+Bb), 90.2 per cent took place in EU countries and 9.8 per cent in EFTA countries. In the EU, again three countries (France, Germany, UK) have a relatively dominant position: France 20.4 per cent of total EU, the UK 16.7 per cent, and Germany 15.6 per cent, a total for the three 52.7 per cent. Of the rest, in a good position are Italy (10 per cent) and Spain (9.1 per cent), followed by Greece (6.9 per cent), the Netherlands (5.5 per cent), Portugal (4.6 per cent), Ireland (4.2 per cent), Belgium (3.6 per cent), Denmark (3.2 per cent) and Luxembourg (0.2 per cent) [Appendix, Table 11(d)].

The flow of transnational student placements, however, affects only a very small proportion of the entire student population in applied sciences. In the academic year 1992/93, for instance, there were approximately 1.8 million higher education students in the EU (12 countries)[14] registered in applied sciences subjects (:mathematics, computer sciences, engineering, architecture), while the Comett programme (1990–94) mobilised only 31655 students, which is just 1.7 per cent of the total.

It is, however, believed that mobility activities, especially student placements, have had a beneficial effect not only on enterprises, where a placement culture is developing which was previously non-existent, but also on students, by becoming better prepared for their professional future, and on higher education institutions, by assisting in awareness building and updating courses and teaching methods[15].

A similar effect is expected from **Eurotecnet**, the action programme designed to promote innovation in the field of vocational training resulting from technological change in the Community. The main actions of the programme (1990–92) included the exchange of information on some 277 innovative training projects initiated by member states and also the dissemination of the results through more than 100 specialised seminars annually. This activity enabled numerous bilateral and multilateral exchanges of scientific specialists (350–400 persons annually) between Eurotecnet projects. The financial means available, however, were very limited: a total MECU 7.1 budget allocation for the period under consideration (Appendix, Table 12).

In the area of **continuing** vocational training, the Community priorities and actions are mainly expressed through the **Force** programme. Of the total amount allocated to this programme (1991–93), the highest proportion (70.9 per cent on average) was directed to Action I which refers to direct projects designed to support innovation in continuing vocational training. A proportion of 19.3 per cent on average was reserved for Action III which encompasses the accompanying measures, such as technical assistance, education and information, and the remaining 9.8 per cent was for Action II which deals with analysis, monitoring, assessment and forecasting (Figure 4.16).

The distribution among the member states is an indication of the degree of national involvement in the programme. Of the total amount allocated, the UK gets the relatively largest proportion (12.7 per cent with 91 projects), followed by Italy (11.6 per cent with 79 projects), Germany (11.5 per cent with 76 projects), Spain (11.4 per cent with 84 projects), France (11.3 per cent with 89 projects), Greece (9.5 per cent

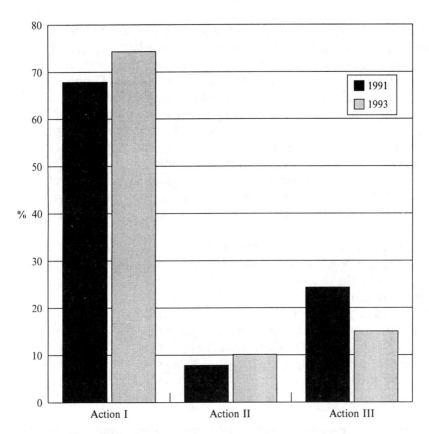

Figure 4.16 Force funding by Action, 1991, 1993 (in %)
Source: Appendix, Table 13(a)

with 72 projects) and Belgium (8.7 per cent with 58 projects). The other member states get smaller proportions [Appendix, Table 13(b)].

It is interesting to mention that the largest proportion of the Force projects were initiated by enterprises or groups of enterprises. Of the total Force projects examined here (720), 36.1 per cent came from enterprises or group of enterprises, as compared with 23.6 per cent for training organisations, 17.4 per cent for other organisations (including universities, training consortia, etc.), 8.3 per cent for employers' organisations, 7.4 per cent for Trade Union organisations, 4.3 per cent for various joint bodies, 2.4 per cent for chambers of commerce and only 0.5 per cent for public authorities [Appendix, Table 13(c)].

(C) Youth: In the youth field, the actions of the Community have mainly been organised through the 'Youth for Europe' programme designed to foster youth exchanges. Of the total amount allocated to the programme (1988–94), approximately 72.6 per cent on average represented direct grants to young people (Action I.1), as compared with 10.1 per cent for the national agencies, 9.0 per cent for European level activities and technical support (Action II), 3.6 per cent for study visits (Action I.3), 3.5 per cent for professional development for youth workers and pilot projects (Action I.4, I.5) and 1.2 per cent for voluntary service (Action I.2) [Appendix, Table 14(a)].

In the Community aid for youth exchanges (Action I.1), the distribution by member states is indicative of the national involvement and the individual preferences of youth. Of the total allocated for Action I.1 (1988–94), Germany gets 15.2 per cent, Italy 13.8 per cent, the UK 12.5 per cent, France 11.4 per cent, and Spain 11.3 per cent, a combined total of 64.2 per cent. Of the other countries, the Netherlands gets 4.9 per cent, Portugal 4.7 per cent, Greece 4.6 per cent, Belgium 3.8 per cent, Denmark 3.0 per cent, Ireland 2.9 per cent, Luxembourg 2.1 per cent, and the remaining 9.8 per cent goes for youth activities at the Community level [Appendix, Table 14(b)]. This distribution of funds resembles the distribution of participants and of projects by member states. Of the total (1674) youth projects adopted in 1993, for example, 34.4 per cent were for the UK with 10016 participants in them, as compared with 12.5 per cent for Spain (with 3672 participants), 11.4 per cent for Germany (with 6933 participants), 10.8 per cent for France (with 5742 participants), 8.2 per cent for Italy (with 3835 participants), 6.0 per cent for Portugal (with 2544 participants), and smaller percentages for the other member states [COM(95) 159 final]. According to EU estimates, the overall participation in the 'Youth for Europe' programme increased from 24000 in 1989 to 40000 in 1993 (Figure 4.17).

The 'Youth for Europe' programme, adopted by the Council on 16 June 1988, is one of the two youth exchange programmes, the other being the 'Young Worker Exchange' programme, which was established in 1964. Their two principal aims are, on the one hand, to enable young people aged between 18 and 28 to complement and enrich their vocational training, and, on the other, to give them the opportunity of participating in the social, cultural and political life of their future partners, the youth of other member states.

There are more than 50 million young people, as here defined, in the Community, which is approximately 15 per cent of the total population. Given that around 10 per cent of the total young people are students in higher education, young workers (full-time, part-time or unemployed) make up the majority of young people aged between 18

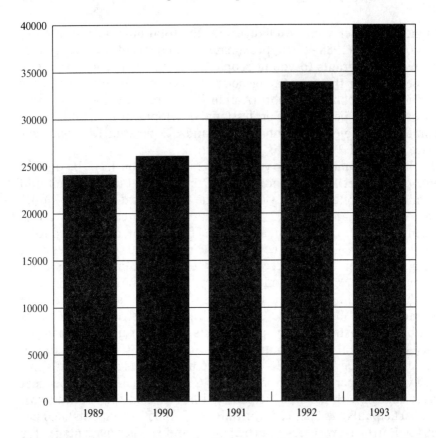

Figure 4.17 Participation in the 'Youth for Europe' programme, 1989–93
Source: EC, 1994, p.31

and 28. Yet the third joint programme on the exchange of young workers got only MECU 32.0 for the period 1985–1991, and managed to
mobilise a total of less than 20000 young workers, which is less than 0.05
per cent of total young workers in the Community [Appendix, Table
15(a)]. Of the total participants in the programme, approximately 20.3
per cent on average were planned for France, as compared with 16.3
per cent for the UK, 12.8 per cent for Italy, 11.2 per cent for Germany,
7.6 per cent for the Netherlands and smaller percentages for the other
member states [Appendix, Table 15(b)].

   In sum there are a few key points that can be drawn from the preceding quantitative analysis of the Community's education and vocational training actions. It is obvious, first of all, that in the field of
education and vocational training the Community acts in accordance

with the principle of subsidiarity whereby actions at the supranational level are mainly aimed at supporting and supplementing the corresponding actions of the member states, while fully respecting the responsibility of the latter for the content and organisation of education and vocational training.

This seemingly democratic sensitivity of the Community has two negative repercussions on the extent and effectiveness of its actions on education and vocational training. One is that the Community's policy on education and training turns out to be a mere embryo of a real policy, for the financial means available for supporting it are very limited. In a budget of approximately 1.06 per cent on average of the Community GDP and around 2.2 per cent on average of public expenditure in the member states, expenditure on education and vocational training is on average less than 7.0 per cent of total Community expenditure (if Social Fund expenditure is included in education and training expenditure).

The second repercussion, which directly derives from the first, is that the Community actions on education and vocational training cannot but affect only a small percentage of the total Community population of youth in general and of pupils, students and academic staff in particular. As a result, the education and vocational training programmes of the Community tend to assume elitist characteristics. From a human capital perspective this means that, taking into account the fact that vocational training assumes priority in the Community actions, the establishment of a single labour market of a highly-skilled labour force is the Community's great concern.

This primacy tends to reinforce the fragmentation of the European labour market for it fosters the establishment of a Community-wide, highly-skilled, labour force, while reproducing the particularities of the traditional labour markets of the member states. To put it differently, the Community's objective, as defined from its education and training measures, centres more on the formation of a limited but highly-skilled European labour force, to meet the needs of the advanced production systems, than on a really integrated labour market, circumscribed by the existing social and regional disparities. I shall argue below that these deficiencies tend to condition the content and the form of the Community's education and vocational training actions.

Notes

1 In 1995, for instance, 74 per cent of ESF financing was for vocational training, as compared with 6 per cent for employment support, 5 per cent for technical assistance and 15 per cent for other support measures. In some countries, like Denmark, Italy, Sweden and the UK, vocational training absorbed around 90 per cent of the corresponding ESF financing [COM(96)502 final].

2 Council Regulation 88/2052/EEC of 24 June 1988 on the tasks of the Structural Funds and their effectiveness and on coordination of their activities between themselves and with the operations of the European Investment Bank and the other existing financial instruments: OJ L185/9, 15. 7. 1988.

3 Council Regulation 88/4255/EEC of 19 December 1988 laying down provisions for implementing Regulation 88/2052/EEC as regards the European Social Fund: OJ L374/21, 31.12. 1988.

4 Council Regulation 93/2081/EEC of 20 July 1993 amending Regulation 88/2052/EEC on the tasks of the Structural Funds and their effectiveness and on coordination of their activities between themselves and with the operations of the European Investment Bank and the other existing financial instruments: OJ L193/5, 31. 7. 1993.

5 Council Regulation 93/2084/EEC of 20 July 1993 amending Regulation 88/4255/EEC laying down provisions for implementing Regulation 88/2052/EEC as regards the European Social Fund: OJ L193/39, 31. 7. 1993.

6 The programme Tempus could also be included in this category, but it does not appear in the EC Budgets from which the statistical information is drawn. It is however analysed below.

7 The analysis which follows goes as far as the statistical information available permits.It should also be mentioned that there is a discrepancy between the statistics drawn from the EC Budgets,which indeed give a clear picture, and those drawn from the Commission's annual reports, which give incomplete information. The reason for the statistical discrepancy may be the difference between appropriations for payments versus outturn in payments and/or the inclusion of additional funds after the approval of the EC Budgets.

8 See Commission of the EC, *Key data on education in the European Union 1995*, p.165.

9 This tendency is further reinforced by the fact that the Erasmus grants cover a relatively small proportion of a student's costs abroad, thereby making it difficult if not impossible for students of low-income families to participate in the programme.

10 Ibid, pp.39, 54.

11 The EC financial support for all these academic initiatives amounts to a total MECU 16.88 for the entire 1990–1996 period (EC Budgets: 1992 to 1996, Subsection B3, Article Item BE-304).

12 cf. COM(93) 704 final, p.17; and Commission of the EC, *Key data on education in the European Union 1995*, p.150.

13 cf. COM(93)704 final, pp.27–30.

14 See Commission of the EC, *Key data on education in the European Union 1995*, p.162.

15 cf. COM(96) 410 final, p.50.

5 The Qualitative Analysis: Deficiencies and Contradictions in EU Education and Training

The preceding analysis has dealt with the Community's competence and actions on education and vocational training. In the overall picture presented one can easily identify certain key policy areas, called in brief 'disputed areas' in education and training policy, which not only tend to define the content and the form of the education and vocational training initiatives of the Community, but also encompass in themselves endemic deficiencies and contradictions. In what follows, I intend to highlight the 'disputed areas' approaching them from three interrelated angles: firstly, from the angle defined by the general debate on the **scope** of European integration in education and training as compared with harmonisation; secondly, from the angle defined by the **content** of this cooperation in the context of the debate between professional activity and academic endeavour; and finally, from the angle of the **efficacy** of this cooperation in the context of the debate on the issue of subsidiarity as a guiding principle in European political integration.

5.1 Harmonisation versus Cooperation

In the area of education and vocational training the Community adopted from the beginning a pragmatic and functional approach to cooperation considering it to be a reflection of progressive harmonisation of economic and social policies. The interesting point is, however, that the Community has in the course of time followed a more or less pragmatic approach to cooperation even in policy areas, such as economic and social policy, where harmonisation was the process stipulated by the treaties. As a result, Community initiatives in education and vocational training tended to lose the functional prerequisite, mentioned above, which could legitimise and reinforce deeper and closer cooperation in the field.

In the area of social policy, for example, the Community quickly shifted from the concept of harmonisation, which entails advanced integration, to those of coordination, cooperation, cohesion or convergence, which allow for greater diversification. Although the EEC Treaty (Article 117, which remained unchanged in the EU Treaty) provided for the harmonisation of social systems, in the context of the functioning of the common market and the improved working conditions and standards of living for workers provided for, in actual practice doubts were expressed about the feasibility or even the desirability of harmonisation (Hantrais, 1995).

The compromise reached called for a more pragmatic and less legalistic approach to cooperation in social policy on the ground that the social dimension of the single market implied not harmonisation but coherence and convergence over a number of precisely defined common objectives. This actually meant, as Hantrais put it, a "lack of commitment to a strongly interventionist social policy founded on the harmonisation of social protection systems". Instead, the member states opted for "cooperation and coordination based on mutual recognition of systems and tolerance of diversity", in the hope of achieving "convergence of national social protection systems", that is, "convergence of goals and policies on the grounds that co-existence of different national systems would enable progress in harmony" (Hantrais, 1995: 20–27).

A similar shift towards a more pragmatic approach to harmonisation occurred in the broader economic area defined by the establishment of the common market. The EEC Treaty calls for the 'approximation' (used interchangeably with 'harmonisation') of the laws of the member states, to the extent required for the proper functioning of the common market [Article 3(h)], and authorises the Council to issue directives for the approximation of such national provisions as directly affect the establishment or functioning of the common market (Article 100).

The objective then was the achievement of a common market rather than a single legal system. In this case harmonisation was to constitute a very relative rendering of laws into Community terms, while respecting the legal order of the member states (Vignes, 1990: 359). In the 1970s the Community moved a step further by adopting a broad definition on harmonisation. Following the rule formulated by the Court of Justice whereby harmonisation was associated with lawful trade and national standards, the Commission advanced the 'mutual acceptance principle' which provides that "goods that have been lawfully produced and marketed in one member state must be allowed in other member states" (Slot, 1996: 380).

This principle, which has also found expression in the field of education and training as indicated below, allowed for a more flexible application of the concept of harmonisation in Community practice. Specifically, in the early period of the Commission's harmonisation programme, total harmonisation was the preferred method. Until the end of 1974, for example, a great part of Community acts involving harmonisation of laws embodied total harmonisation. This meant that member states were given insufficient powers and flexibility to regulate at national level. The result was that the method of total harmonisation fell out of favour with member states, and more flexible schemes were introduced. One was the optional harmonisation, which was the favourite method in the early 1970s, whereby the manufacturer of goods was given the option to follow either the harmonised rules or the national rules. The second method, which became important in the late 1970's and the 1980's, was the minimum harmonisation method 'allowing for upward flexibility at a national level and referring to specific areas such as, eg. consumer protection, environment and public health. And finally, the third method was based on the principle of 'mutual recognition of national rules', on the ground that what constitutes, for example, a safe and healthy product should in principle not be much different from one member state to another. The general system for the recognition of higher education diplomas, to which I return below, is an example of this type of harmonisation (Slot, 1996: 382–88; Vignes, 1990: 364–67; Pelkmans, 1987; Barry, 1994).

These developments imply that when the Community actually decided, in the 1970s onwards, to deal with the issue of education and training, the general climate had already shifted towards a more pragmatic approach to harmonisation and cooperation. Thus it is with no surprise that even in the field of vocational training, about which the EEC Treaty contains specific provisions (Articles 118 & 128), the Community's initial actions were mere suggestions for cooperation. The Council Decision of 2 April 1963, which outlined general principles for implementing a common vocational training policy, authorised the Community to frame a common vocational training policy so as to enable levels of training to be harmonised progressively. However, the main programmes introduced for that purpose (Petra, Force, Comett, Eurotecnet, Leonardo) identify as their main aim to support and complement the policies and activities developed by the member states in the area of vocational training. The Leonardo programme in particular, which was adopted on the basis of the provisions of the EU Treaty (Article 127), states clearly that the Treaty does give the Community the responsibility of implementing a vocational training policy. This however is done on the condition that the policy should be implemented while fully respecting the responsibility of the member states for the content and organisation of vocational training, and excludes any harmonisation of the laws and regulations of the member states.

The area of education proper, on the other hand, remained a taboo subject for the Community at least up until the early 1970s. The first meeting in Council of the ministers of education took place in 1971 wherein the ministers recognised the need to establish a basis for cooperation in the field of education. Two years later (1973) education was included for the first time in the services of the Community (DGXII) as a policy area, together with research and science policy (Neave, 1984: 6–8; McMahon, 1995: 13–14). This meant that the Community continued at that time to uphold the traditional distinction between education and vocational training, where the former maintained a more academic orientation.

In this context, the Council Resolution of 1974 established the basic principles of cooperation in education[1]. These included (i) the achievement of equal opportunity for free access to all forms of education, (ii) the importance of upholding the diversity and particular character of member state education systems (implying that 'educational cooperation had to make allowance for the traditions of each country and the diversity of their respective educational policies and systems' and that, therefore, 'harmonisation of these systems could not be considered an end in itself'), and thus (iii) the separation between objectives and means: cooperation was to involve the statement of specific objectives as part of Community policy, while the application of these objectives was left to the member states.

The objectives of the Community programme on cooperation in education were initially set by the Council Resolution of 1976 which established education as a concurrent responsibility by specifying actions to be carried out at Community level and those falling under national responsibility[2]. This 'dual' nature of the 1976 Resolution, as Neave put it (Neave, 1984: 10–11), has now found legal expression in the principle of subsidiarity to be discussed below.

The interesting point here is that the initial position of the Community to view education mostly in the context of its academic qualities did not last for very long. Faced with deep economic crisis and high levels of

unemployment, the Community opted in the early 1980s for a more functional and integrated approach to education and training. This development found expression in the very organisation of the Community
where education and vocational training became directly associated with
social policy under the same Directorate General (DGV). In this sense
education and vocational training were subordinated to social policy
objectives, and the employment-related goals of educational policy
remained of paramount importance for the Community even when, in
the 1990s, a separate Directorate General (DGXXII) was established for
education, training and youth (McMahon, 1995: 12–14).

In educational cooperation, the underlying theme of the integrated
approach to education and training was the so-called 'convergence
thesis', which implied that "as the economies of different countries come
to resemble one another, so the solutions sought in the educational field
will follow a broadly similar path" (Neave, 1984: 165). This in turn could
lead to what some analysts have called 'hidden harmonisation', that is,
a sort of "gradual convergence of culture and fashion, of social habit
and intellectual trend, of rule and regulation, of convention and practice common across all member states" (Hopkins et al, 1994: 18).

The fact remains, however, that cooperation in education and vocational training in the Community, as it stands today, could at best
encourage the 'voluntary' harmonisation of aspects of national educational policy, through the grant of financial aid by the Community
(Lenaerts, 1994: 35). This pragmatic, step-by-step approach to cooperation defines all the Community initiatives on education. In all
Community programmes on education proper (e.g. Erasmus, Lingua,
Socrates) the 'dual' principle on cooperation is upheld and the national
responsibility is respected. This is best illustrated in the Socrates programme, established following the provisions of the EU Treaty (Article
126), where the Community confines itself to contributing to the development of quality education by encouraging cooperation between member states and, if necessary, by supporting and supplementing their
action, while fully respecting the responsibility of the member states for
the content of teaching and the organisation of education systems and
their cultural and linguistic diversity. This non-harmonisation provision,
which is associated with the principle of subsidiarity, appears to be, in
the words of Sprokkereef, "the price paid for including education in the
treaty, as several national delegations were very concerned about the
possible effects of its incorporation" (Sprokkereef, 1995: 345).

In the Community practice, therefore, cooperation in education and
vocational training should be interpreted in the context of a field of pos-

sibilities whose limits are defined by two distinct but interrelated views: (i) the **pragmatic** view according to which cooperation stands as an instrument through which member states, without releasing their national jurisdiction, simply try to pool knowledge on how to deal with educational questions; and (ii) the **normative** view wherein cooperation in education is seen as a necessary step towards the construction of a new Europe (cf. Neave, 1984: 200–201).

The analysis thus far suggests that on education and vocational training the Community actually oscillates between these two distinct possibilities, having placed more emphasis on the 'pragmatic' approach to educational cooperation. To the extent then that the declared objective towards political union in Europe remains valid, the pragmatic approach to educational cooperation becomes not only deficient but mainly contradictory. Here, Jean Monnet's confession that, given the opportunity to create the European Community again, he would take education as a starting point (Sprokkereef, 1995: 340), assumes its real significance. I shall argue below that these deficiencies and contradictions as regards the **scope** of European cooperation in education and training tend to undermine the **content** of this cooperation as exemplified by the debate on academic endeavour and professional activity.

5.2   Academic versus Professional

The discussion here unfolds the essence of the education and vocational training initiatives of the Community, and centres on three interrelated issues: (a) the issue of the recognition of diplomas or other qualifications, (b) the issue of vocational training as compared with education proper, and (c) the issue of higher education as compared with traditional university education.

(A) The mutual recognition of qualifications, stipulated in the Community treaties, exemplifies the shift from harmonisation to cooperation. The Treaty (Article 57 EC) authorised the Council to issue directives for the mutual recognition of diplomas, certificates and other evidence of formal qualifications, in order to make it easier for persons to take up and pursue activities in the single market. In this sense, the mutual recognition of qualifications, being directly associated with the functioning of the common labour market, had to deal with the common requirements for **professional** recognition.

These requirements include periods of training, membership in professional associations, experience, and education diploma or certificate.

This means that the professional recognition of qualifications is a process which endemically encompasses elements of academic nature, as regards the content and organisation of education, which themselves point to a parallel **academic** recognition of qualifications. In fact, as Lenaerts points out, the Community initially took the view that the professional recognition of diplomas, certificates and other evidence of formal qualifications "also hinges on the harmonisation of training curricula" (Lenaerts, 1994: 16).

The sectoral approach to the professional recognition of qualifications, which was initially adopted by the Community, reflected these very concerns on the interdependence between professional recognition and coordination of training curricula. This approach was destined to encounter in practice serious difficulties for two main reasons: first, because it was introduced during a period when the principle of harmonisation tended to lose political legitimacy in the Community. In this sense, Funnel and Muller argue, the failure to "agree harmonised qualifications" can be seen as part of the wider set of problems associated with "all forms of harmonisation" which "moved politically and pragmatically to the development of a single market based on the mutual recognition of standards" (Funnel and Muller, 1991: 68). The second reason was the absence of a historical prospect in the sectoral approach to the recognition of qualifications: unable or unwilling to deal with key academic aspects of the education process, the Community actually tried to solve the problem of the recognition of qualifications in a conjunctural manner, thus reproducing the very obstacles to harmonisation which emanated from the educational diversity of the member states.

The general approach to the professional recognition of qualifications, which followed, represented an effort on the part of the Community not only to bypass altogether the issue of harmonisation but also to separate professional recognition from academic recognition. The notion of recognition was here associated with that of mutual trust set on the ground of excluding the principle of equivalence of study programmes. The principle of mutual trust was based on the questionable assumption that certificates awarded in the member states are basically comparable and that the levels of training in the Community countries are of high standard (Laslet, 1990). This move towards general recognition clearly lessens the direct Community impact on national educational systems which, assumed comparable, no longer need be coordinated, let alone harmonised (Lonbay, 1989).

It is in this context that one must evaluate the significance, if any, of the Community pronouncements on academic recognition, drawn on the experience of other international organisations. Whereas professional recognition of qualifications is the recognition for the purpose of taking up professional activities, academic recognition is the recognition of education entrance qualifications, study periods, intermediate and final qualifications (e.g. certificates, diplomas), which normally take place inside the education institutions and is directed at taking up or continuing studies (Dalichow, 1987: 56).

The Council of Europe and UNESCO have both established multilateral conventions covering (i) the equivalence of diplomas leading to admission to universities, (ii) the equivalence of periods of university study, and (iii) the academic recognition of university qualifications. All these conventions, however, are political instruments and thus their success largely depends on the goodwill of the member states or institutions (Dalichow, 1987). It is for this reason that it has been argued that both in the area of academic recognition and in the field of academic mobility the Community has far outstripped the Council of Europe (Hagen, 1987).

In 1974 the Community expressed the wish that future work on the mutual recognition of diplomas, certificates and other evidence of formal qualifications be guided by the desire for a flexible and qualitative approach, and promised improved possibilities for academic recognition of diplomas and periods of study[3]. This entailed, according to the 1976 action programme in the field of education, evaluation of the situation with regard to the academic recognition of diplomas with the aim of developing a network of agreements, and consultations between the member states to facilitate the recognition of periods of study and studies carried out[4].

The JSP scheme (Joint Programmes of Study), the SSV scheme (Short Study Visits), and the NARIC network (National Academic Recognition Information Centres), introduced in 1976, 1977, and 1984 respectively, were measures to facilitate the academic recognition of diplomas and periods of study. All these measures later became integral parts of the Community education programmes, in which the ECTS scheme (Community Course Credit Transfer System) was also incorporated (Dalichow, 1987; Hagen, 1987).

Academic recognition of periods of study thus became a prerequisite for the operation of the education programmes of the Community. What this means is that academic recognition as here perceived necessarily affects only a small proportion of the entire student population of the Community, those participating in the EC education programmes. And this participation, as Dalichow reminds us, is deficient within the member states of the Community, "in part because academic recognition of higher education entrance qualifications, study periods, intermediate and final examinations is not automatic between EC countries". This is because, Dalichaw adds, "mutual trust and confidence in the quality of higher education within other member states is lacking, equity is asked for instead of equivalence" (Dalichaw, 1987: 55–56).

Thus viewed, the conclusion is that a genuine policy on academic recognition requires at least a minimum of harmonisation among the member states on those key elements which define academic recognition itself. Furthermore, the artificial distinction between academic recognition and professional recognition, which exists in Community practice despite its pronouncements on the 'synergy' between 'academic' and 'professional' [cf. COM(96)46 final], tends to undermine European political integration by emphasising the professional character of education (i.e., vocational education and training as a requirement for the 'traders' Europe') to the detriment of the academic character of education (i.e., education proper as a requirement for the 'people's Europe').

(B) The emphasis on vocational education and training was in fact the logical outcome of the very legal provisions of the Community, which excluded general education from its jurisdiction up until the signing of the EU Treaty. Thus the Community was destined to oscillate between the traditional view, on the one hand, based on the dichotomy between general education and vocational training, and the contemporary view, on the other, considering general education and vocational training as a single totality. In either case, the Community objective was simple and clear: to foster the development of a single labour market and advance the qualities of Community human capital.

In the initial period (1963 to 1976), according to Neave, EC policy development towards vocational training tended to follow the traditional dichotomy between general education and vocational training. It was a period defined by the 1963 Council Decision on the general principles for implementing a common vocational training policy, and the 1976 Council Resolution on an action programme in the field of education. Then, under the force of the growing youth unemployment, the Community moved towards a more integrated approach on general education and vocational training. The reason for this was, as Neave put it, that "the quantitative problems of moving from school form to factory involved not merely the nature of vocational training itself, but also its place in the broader structures of the education system as a whole" (Neave, 1984: 65).

This integrated but market-oriented approach to general education and vocational training was further reinforced by the Community through the incorporation in 1981 of education and training into the general field of social policy and employment. In this way the Community consciously tried to break down the barriers between general education and vocational training, with the ultimate aim of developing a 'technological culture' conducive to the formation of a highly skilled and well-educated labour force (Fogg and Jones, 1985; Freedland, 1996: 117).

The underlying assumption in this widely-held view is that the economic challenges faced by the advanced industrial societies require structural adjustments and rapid technological development wherein lifelong learning becomes pivotal to contemporary progress. In this context, the traditional distinctions between general education and vocational training are thought to disappear "as all programmes are confronted with the need to develop both theoretical content and relevance to future occupational and educational careers" (OECD, 1992: 32–34).

The deficiency in this proposition is not on the relevance of education to social and economic development, about which there is general agreement, but on the assumed direct correlation between education and training objectives and labour market needs. This assumed correlation is actually problematic for a number of reasons and most importantly because it is extremely difficult to make reliable manpower forecasting and also to predict with accuracy the future 'needs' of the economy (Kokulsing et al, 1996: 20–29; Hussain, 1976).

The interesting point here is that the Community, having assumed that the said correlation is accurate, tried to cultivate a market-oriented approach to education questions, including higher education itself considered to be education for vocational training. The definition on vocational training given by the Court of Justice, according to which any form of education which prepares for a particular profession or employment is vocational training, became *ipso facto* the point of reference for Community action in the field of education. In retrospect, the Court's definition carried with it a positive effect for it helped to strengthen Community competence in education, thereby stimulating further integration. If approached from a different angle, however, one can argue that the Court's definition gave legitimacy to the Community's utilitarian approach to education, thereby creating much confusion on the value of the humanitarian and critical objectives of education, and also established a precedent on the instrumental role of the judicial power in

European integration to the detriment of the democratic process itself (cf. McMahon, 1995: 95).

All the education and training programmes of the Community are greatly conditioned by this utilitarian principle aimed at contributing to the development of quality education and training and the creation of an open European area for cooperation in education and training. The EU Treaty does give the space, especially through the provisions of Article 126 on the development of quality education, for a broader view on education and training, but this possibility is actually circumscribed by two main factors: (i) the principle of subsidiarity, to be discussed below, which tends to confine EU action on education and training to a very narrow space so as to only 'encourage', 'support' or 'supplement' the actions of the member states, and (ii) the utilitarian principle which tends to dominate Community thinking on education and training.

This is best exemplified by the Commission White Paper on education and training entitled 'Teaching and Learning: Towards the learning society' [COM(95)590] which declares the end of the debates on educational principles and the subjection of general education objectives to the requirements of vocational training. This is because, the Commission report states, a "broad knowledge base and training for employment are no longer two contradictory or separate things", since there is "increasing recognition for the importance of general knowledge in using vocational skills" [COM(95)590, p.42].

The Community cannot claim originality in using the concept of 'learning society', for the term was introduced in 1983 by the USA Government in a report on excellence in education. The report stated that in a world of "ever-accelerating competition and change in the conditions of the workplace", education "should focus on the goal of creating a Learning Society". In such a society, the report adds, the underlying principle must be "the commitment to a set of values and to a system of education that affords all members the opportunity to stretch their minds to full capacity, from early childhood through adulthood, learning more as the world changes" (USA, 1983: 13–15 quoted in Kokulsing et al, 1996: 6).

The idea was then adopted by the Confederation of British Industry in 1991 and endorsed by the British Government at the beginning of the 1990s in an effort to turn Britain into 'a learning society' by the year 2000. This entailed a process of 'skills revolution' aimed at creating 'a new training culture' so as to empower individuals with 'real buying power' for 'career mobility and needs satisfaction' (Kokulsing et al, 1996: 5–16). Similarly, for the OECD officials, like their counterparts in the

EU, this very 'skills revolution', reinforced by the imperatives of the information technologies, implied the rediscovery of human resources as a prime catalyst to successful economic and social change (Papadopoulos, 1994; IRDAC, 1994)[5].

Thus posed, education in the Community was destined to serve the needs and requirements of vocational training with the ultimate aim of producing a highly skilled and qualified labour force, thereby increasing productivity and strengthening international competitiveness. I shall argue below that this mainly utilitarian approach to education also tends to define the content of university education itself, perceived now within the broader notion of higher education.

(C) The Community consistently employs the notion of 'higher education', while referring not only to traditional universities but also to other educational institutions with at least a three-year programme, although it is a notion less homogeneous that might appear at first glance (Smith, 1985). For example, the resolution of 1974 on cooperation in the field of education called for 'increased cooperation between institutions of higher education', while the Resolution of 1976 on an action programme in the field of education underlined the need 'to promote cooperation in the field of higher education'. Similarly, the Parliament Resolution of 1984 considered the 'growing importance of the debate on the identity of the Community' and the role which higher education should play in the development of a 'European awareness among the citizens of the Community', and called for 'the development of cooperation between higher education establishments'[6].

The major education programmes of the Community use the terms 'university' and 'higher education institution' interchangeably. For example, the Comett programme was introduced to strengthen and encourage 'cooperation between universities and enterprises', while the Erasmus programme was set up to enhance the mobility of 'university students' and generally to 'promote greater cooperation between universities'. The term 'university', however, was used to cover 'all types of post-secondary education and training establishments' which offer 'qualifications or diplomas of that level', whatever such establishments may be called in the member states. In this context, Council Directive 89/48/EEC called for the recognition of 'higher education diplomas' awarded on completion of professional education and training 'of at least three years' duration' at 'a university or establishment of higher education or another establishment of similar level'[7].

The Commission memorandum on higher education in the EC called for intensified cooperation between 'higher education institutions' defined so as to cover both universities, including those engaged in research based teaching, as well as 'all other post-secondary establishments of education and training' which offer courses of varying duration and of either a general or specialised nature leading to qualifications of a post-secondary level [COM(91)349]. Similarly, the Council conclusions of 27 November 1992 called for the development of 'the European dimension in higher education', underlining that the Comett, Erasmus, Lingua, and Tempus programmes, for example, have become 'distinctive features of the life of higher education institutions in the Community and beyond' (OJ C334, 19.12.1992). Finally, the umbrella programmes of 'Leonardo' and 'Socrates' leave no doubt that the term 'university' is understood in EC practice to mean 'all types of higher education institutions which offer qualifications or diplomas at that level, regardless of how such establishments are referred to in the member states[8].

This general approach to 'higher education' seems to represent a policy of convenience for the Community and the member states, for it allows for the largest possible participation of 'higher education' institutions in the Community's education programmes. The deficiency here is, however, that this 'equalisation' of 'higher education' institutions tends to undermine both the content and the quality of 'higher education' itself. This is because, first, the 3-year minimum requirement set by the Community for the inclusion of an institution into the 'higher education' category cannot by itself guarantee Community-wide equality (let alone quality) in post-secondary education institutions, when the duration in basic education (primary and secondary) varies among the member states. In the EU15, basic education (primary and secondary) ends at the age of 18 in 7 member states (Belgium, Greece, Spain, France, Netherlands, Portugal, UK), and at the age of 19 in the remaining 8 member states. This variation tends to affect the minimum duration of study for a first degree university diploma, which mainly varies from 3 to 4 years (European Commission, 1995).

Furthermore, the said 'equalisation' of 'higher education' institutions rests on slippery grounds by ignoring the fact that by definition there is a qualitative difference between university education and non-university education. For, whereas the latter primarily aims to provide theoretical and practical education in the arts and sciences and their application to professional activities, university education aims to ensure a sound scientific and cultural preparation for the reproduction of knowledge, by fostering the development of abilities related to thinking, innovation and critical analysis. The Community's utilitarian approach to education tends to wipe out these qualitative differences and thus to legitimise

claims for the transformation of non-university higher education institutions into universities, as was the case with the British Polytechnics[9],
to the detriment of the quality of 'higher education' itself.

This happens at a time when the university is forced, under the cir-
cumstances, to strengthen the quality of its cultural product, remove
the barriers weaved by nationalism, and enter the stage of international
competition and cooperation (Papadopoulos, 1994; Brock and
Tulasiewicz, 1994; Lenzen, 1996). In simple words, the new international
dimensions and perspectives which arise from the growing interdependence of countries make imperative the cooperation in education. In
the EU context, I shall argue below that this cooperation is circumscribed
by the existing divergence between economic integration and political
union.

5.3   Political versus Economic

The principle of subsidiarity was envisaged to respond to the discrepancy existing between 'political' and 'economic', by supposedly defining
the political content of European integration. In it, there is an expression not only of a **fear** that the Community may arrogate excessive competence, but also of a **hope** that subsidiarity itself will operate as a
safeguard against a unilateral expansion of supranational powers
(Emiliou, 1992).

In a sense, subsidiarity becomes a Janus-faced concept capable of
either supporting or undermining the legitimacy of EU policy. For, it
may operate either as an instrument of the member states to protect their
own interests, or as an instrument of sub-national actors to challenge
the national centre, or even as an EU instrument to increase activities
in previously excluded areas of policy. It all depends on the interpreta-
tion given in a specific historical conjuncture conditioned by the interplay of interests, actors and ideologies (Van Kersbergen and Verbeek,
1994; Golub, 1996).

In the political context of federalism, where the concept can be fully
understood and defined, subsidiarity tends to play a dual role: one, as a
criterion for the division of competences between the different levels of
political power; and another, as a means to delineate the dividing line
between the individual sphere and that of the state, thereby defining
political rights, be they individual or group rights, and responsibilities.
The concept historically stems from Catholic social doctrine according
to which society exists for the individual and not the opposite. In the

context of the EU the concept of subsidiarity has been used as a substantive principle and as a procedural criterion: the former means that subsidiarity becomes a tool to enhance the Community's democratic legitimacy and close its 'democratic deficit', whereas the latter entails a division of policy-making responsibilities to achieve efficiency. In this last capacity, subsidiarity becomes the vehicle to justify both public intervention and the withdrawal of state activity (Van Kersbergen and Verbeek, 1994; Kuhnhart, 1991; Harrison, 1996). In a neo-liberal context, this last possibility means that state or EC action tends to be subordinated to the requirements of a single market strategy and the neo-liberal approach to social organisation and economic competitiveness. The consequences of this possibility for education and training policy will be clarified shortly, following a further explanation of the principle of subsidiarity in the EU context.

In the intergovernmental conferences which preceded the agreement on the EU Treaty, the Commission took the position that the principle of subsidiarity, associated with the redefinition of some of the Community's powers, had to be used as a guiding principle so as to secure that the exercise of power does not become an abuse of power (Commission of the EC, 1991). In keeping with this logic the EU Treaty stipulates that, in areas which do not fall within its exclusive competence, the Community takes action, 'in accordance with the principle of subsidiarity', only if the objectives of the proposed action cannot be sufficiently achieved by the member states and can therefore, by 'reason of the scale or effects of the proposed action', be better achieved by the Community (Article 3b). Education and vocational training is such an area and thus the Community only encourages cooperation between member states and supports and supplements their action, while fully respecting the responsibility of the member states for the content of teaching and the organisation of education systems and their cultural and linguistic diversity (Articles 126 & 127)[10].

It is this very need to preserve the 'cultural and linguistic diversity' throughout the Community which reinforces national jurisdiction on education. The member states are not prepared to abandon those features of education which they regard as essential to the promotion of a national ethos (Holmes, 1992). Underneath this legitimate reason, however, there are more serious concerns on the part of the member states which tend to put obstacles to a genuine cooperation in education.

It is, first of all, the concern about the **socialisation** function of education and its impact on social cohesion and political legitimisation. The education systems are by their nature destined to reproduce certain dominant values in society, through the curricula of schools and higher education institutions, thereby mediating both political power and ethnocentrism. The latter tends to become a convenient means not only of cultivating 'national identity' but mainly of sustaining 'political power' at the national level. The by-product of this political necessity is the reproduction, especially in periods of economic decline, of both covert and overt expressions of xenophobia and racism, both in schools and universities and in the wider society that these institutions serve (Coulby and Jones, 1995).

It is, secondly, the concern about the financial costs of education and the unwillingness of member states to strengthen the social dimension of the single market which includes the funding of education as well. The declared objective of the Community to contribute to the development of 'quality education' becomes an empty phrase unless the necessary financial support is given to (the primarily most needed) member states to introduce the improvements required. A genuine cooperation in education, based on common objectives and sound EU funding, will certainly enhance quality education in such key areas as, for instance, the infrastructure of the education systems, the ratio between students and teachers, the enlargement of pre-school education, the length of compulsory schooling, the nature of upper secondary level education and training, the structure and content of university higher education, and the teaching of foreign languages (cf. Hantrais, 1995: 52–56). In areas such as these, the absence of financial means makes meaningless and in a way hypocritical the statement that the Community aims to develop 'quality education', but, in accordance with the principle of subsidiarity, it can only 'encourage, facilitate, stimulate, supplement' the actions of the member states, while fully respecting national responsibility on education. The thing which is missing here is the willingness and political commitment to establish a genuine European **social** community[11].

This brings us to the third reason, which is the concern about European political union itself. The insistence on the 'national jurisdiction' over education questions tends to become here a convenient alibi for the unwillingness of member states to commit themselves to a European political project. This is best exemplified by the fact that the principle of subsidiarity tends to receive conflicting interpretations: either (i) as a driving principle towards the formation of a truly federal political system in the European Union, or (ii) as a political framework aiming at the establishment of a loose con-federal political system resembling an inter-governmental decision-making structure, or even (iii) as a policy mainly directed towards the political legitimisation of the neo-liberal strategy aiming at the privatisation of the social costs (cf. Van Kersbergen and Verbeek, 1994; Teasdale, 1993).

This means that, whilst the establishment of a single market (:economic integration) has sustained a Community-wide support, the formation of a social and political community (:political integration) continues to remain an object of dispute among the member states. This in turn has reinforced the option for a differentiated Community (Stubb, 1996), itself rationalised in terms of variations in economic performance among member states, which means that the level of power at which decision-making will be effective will ultimately vary not only from country to country, but also from subject to subject. In this context, the real question is, as Marquand put it, "how much diversity an emerging political union can stand without dissolving into its constituent parts" (Marquand, 1994: 26). This question, which obviously cannot be answered a priori, leads to the conclusion that in the end the pace of political integration cannot but influence the content and the form of the Community's policies, including that on education and vocational training.

Notes

1 Resolution of the Ministers for Education meeting within the Council of 6 June 1974 on cooperation in the field of education: OJ C98, 20. 8. 1974. See also Neave, 1984: 9–10.
2 Resolution of the Council and of the Ministers for Education meeting within the Council of 9 February 1976 comprising an action programme in the field of education: OJ C38, 19. 2. 1976. See also Neave, 1984: 10–11; and McMahon, 1995: 10–11.
3 See Council resolution of 6 June 1974 on the mutual recognition of diplomas, certificates and other evidence of formal qualifications: OJ C98, 20. 8. 1974; and Resolution of the Ministers for Education meeting within the Council of 6 June 1974 on cooperation in the field of education: OJ C98, 20. 8. 1974.
4 See Resolution of the Council and of the Ministers for Education meeting within the Council of 9 February 1976 comprising an action programme in the field of education: OJ C38, 19. 2. 1976.
5 The same concerns also appear in the recent report to UNESCO of the International Commission on Education for the Twenty-first Century (Delors et al, 1996).
6 See OJ C98, 20. 8. 1974; OJ C38, 19. 2. 1976; and OJ C104, 16. 4. 1984.
7 See OJ C222, 8. 8. 1986; OJ L166, 25. 6. 1987; and OJ L19, 24. 1. 1989.
8 See OJ L340, 29. 12. 1994, and OJ L87, 20. 4. 1995.
9 This was the result of the pronouncements of Margaret Thatcher and her Ministers that Britain had too many social scientists and too few engineers, and that therefore the educational system had to develop more vocationally relevant curricula, thereby fostering the utilitarianism of education (Roots, 1996).
10 In the context of subsidiarity, a distinction is being made between 'exclusive powers' and 'concurrent or shared powers': the former refer to the implementation of the four

economic freedoms of movement, while the latter refer to the accompanying measures which are designed to facilitate the operation of the internal market. Thus the competence of the Community in education and training is conditioned by the relevance of this policy area to the functioning of the common market [COM(93)545; and COM(94)533].

11 It is not surprising, therefore, that member states such as UK, for instance, approve Community action on education only on the condition that Community expenditure on education and training is contained (See, for instance, Select Committee on European Legislation, HC48-ii, HC48-xiii, HC48-xvii, HC48-xviii, HC48-xix, HC48-xx).

6 Epilogue

The central theme developed in this work is that the Community, being mainly defined by the requirements of economic integration, has followed a utilitarian approach to education and training conducive to the 'good' functioning of the common market. This implies that education and training in the Community primarily aims to facilitate the reproduction of the labour force in an integrated labour market. The reason being that, as Lowe has emphatically stressed, all the member states of the Community perceive two things: one is "a causal relationship between the quality and level of their national education and training provision and the efficiency of their economies"; and the other is "the necessity of competing with Japan, the United States, and the newly industrialised countries of Asia and Latin America by ensuring that such provision is geared to the needs of modern societies". For this reason they are interested in any kind of "European cooperation designed to exploit human resources to the full and, explicitly, to facilitate the transition of young people from education to paid employment" (Lowe, 1992: 582).

The education and training programmes of the Community are designed to mainly respond to this objective. The weaknesses involved in these programmes are twofold: one is the **economic** discrepancy between the limited financial resources supplied through these programmes and the growing needs of the member states for the improvement of the qualities of human capital and the reproduction of the labour force. The other is the **structural** discrepancy between the unified rules of operation of the education programmes and the uneven development of the member states of the Community. These discrepancies combined tend to reproduce existing regional and social inequalities thereby perpetuating the fragmentation of the European labour market.

The perpetuation of this social question tends to condition the cultural-political dimension of education. The discrepancy here is between the programmatic declarations of the Community for the enhancement of the so called quality education at the European level and the unwillingness of the member states to denationalise the jurisdiction on education. A good example of this is the contradictory stand of the national authorities on two interrelated objectives: the recognition of certificates

95

and diplomas at the Community level, as a prerequisite for the establishment of a European labour market and the cultivation of a broader common understanding, and the assessment of the quality of the national education systems, as a precondition for the recognition itself of certificates and diplomas. While the member states are inclined to eventually agree on common Community rules for the recognition of certificates and diplomas, they seem unwilling to give their consent for Community intervention in the evaluation of their education systems and institutions. I have argued in this work that these discrepancies cannot easily be solved as long as the **political** form of the European Union remains an open question.

This direct correlation between education and European integration brings to the fore the broader theoretical question on the relationship between EU education and training initiatives and theories of integration. The question was recently raised by Beukel (1994) in an article on the relevance of the neo-functionalist theoretical paradigm to educational developments in the Community. The essence of the article's argument is that the cooperation in the EC on aspects of education cannot be explained in neo-functionalist terms whereby integration in one sector is considered to have an inherently expansive character, encapsulated in the 'spill-over' concept. In Beukel's words, "neither a functional nor a cultivated 'spill-over' notion yields a valid explanation for the higher level of integration since the mid-1980s" in the field of education. And "neither can it be explained by focusing on the Community's original economic-political aim of establishing a common market", or even "by the activities of the Commission as the Community's primary supranational institution" (Beukel, 1994: 45).

Rather, Beukel argues, the dynamics of the higher levels of integration in the educational field have to be looked for by examining 'environmental factors', both economic and political, which are "beyond the establishment of the common market and beyond the objectives and activities of the Community's most prominent supranational institution"(p.46). The economic factors relate to the process of globalisation of the economies and the subsequent transformation from 'industrial society to the information society'. In this sense, "the Community's new educational initiatives are closely related to the growth of the information society" (p.48)[1]. This in turn, says Beukel, has helped to create favourable political conditions conducive to Community initiatives in education: "the growing quest and support for a European cultural and political identity", coupled with "the related greater interest for Europe's role in relation to the United States and the Soviet Union", implied in the 1980s "a positive pre-attitude to educational cooperation in the Community"(p.49).

The weakness in Beukel's argument is that he tends to consider these 'environmental factors' as being 'external' to the very logic of European integration and thus to distance himself from the reasoning of neo-functionalism towards which his criticisms are directed. How else can one interpret his conclusion that the "growth and development of education as a Community issue was not simply an effect determined by the initiation and implementation of the common market project", and thus "the integration of general education in the EC cannot be explained in terms of the functional 'spill-over' concept"(p.49)[2].

The argument advanced in this work is that the education and training initiatives of the Community are expressions of a dual necessity: One, to foster the process of capital accumulation through the improvement of the qualities of human capital; and second, to create conditions conducive to political legitimisation through the enhancement of a European identity. The primacy of economic integration in the EC construction has reinforced a utilitarian approach to education and training, whereas the uncertainty of political integration has circumscribed the prospects of cooperation in education. Political integration is still 'a journey to an unknown destination' (Taylor, 1996: 58), that is, a variable condition defined by the minimalist threshold which demarcates integration from mere intergovernmental cooperation, and the maximalist outcome with the creation of a new political unity (O'Neill, 1996: 12).

In this space of possibilities, the content and the form of the Community's initiatives on education and training tend to represent the political outcome of an unstable compromise[3]: 'compromise' because the very existence of the EU requires political accommodation of diverging interests in a symbiotic relationship between the growth of the Community and the nation state; and 'unstable' because the very limits of the compromise itself are defined by the political conjuncture. This is why the pace of political integration ultimately conditions the Community's competence in the field of education.

Notes

1 The same argument appears in the Commission's White Paper on education and training [COM(95)590 final].
2 The inconsistencies of neo-functionalism and of the broader conventional theoretical approaches to integration are now a well-established fact, cf. O'Neill, 1996; Moschonas, 1996.
3 cf. Poulantzas, 1975 as regards the concept of 'unstable compromise'.

Appendix

Table 1   Community revenue, 1987–1996 (in MECU – current prices)

	1987	1988	1989	1990	1991	1992	1993	1994	1995	1996
Total, of which:	36313.4	41843.4	45899.8	46469.1	56249.2	59711.8	65672.7	70013.5	75077.1	81888.4
Belgium (B)	1631.2	1833.5	1807.2	1763.7	2217.4	2239.1	2536.1	2763.9	2666.9	3106.9
Denmark (DK)	809.3	955.6	871.0	775.1	1033.5	1034.8	1216.9	1376.7	1283.5	1564.4
Germany (D)	9464.5	11534.9	11110.4	10357.5	15394.2	16997.5	18697.9	21100.3	20611.9	24420.8
Greece (GR)	474.7	429.9	566.3	563.6	762.1	728.6	923.0	1019.1	992.2	1196.5
Spain (E)	3023.1	2678.1	3575.1	3671.4	4580.2	4828.0	5669.6	5654.1	4409.1	5188.3
France (F) ·	6904.4	9095.4	8622.8	8089.1	10601.9	10493.4	12088.9	13442.5	12443.7	14338.3
Ireland (IRL)	404.6	328.2	370.9	368.5	452.4	462.3	519.7	542.5	788.1	767.6
Italy (I)	4974.4	5426.7	7605.9	6097.7	8699.7	8279.9	10292.6	9843.3	7992.5	9868.8
Luxembourg (L)	66.5	81.6	72.8	74.5	108.8	123.5	125.0	148.7	155.6	183.1
Netherlands (NL)	2279.5	2795.6	2700.5	2615.2	3537.7	3534.0	4090.5	4379.1	4113.7	4729.0
Austria (A)	–	–	–	–	–	–	–	–	1884.4	2348.8
Portugal (P)	384.8	399.9	458.3	502.4	712.0	838.1	1023.6	1139.5	1033.8	1212.3
Finland (FIL)	–	–	–	–	–	–	–	–	951.3	1239.1
Sweden (S)	–	–	–	–	–	–	–	–	1719.1	2340.4
United Kingdom (UK)	5622.2	5323.9	6568.1	6534.3	4736.4	6702.4	7880.6	8087.4	9198.3	8816.1
Other [1]	273.6	960.1	1570.5	5056.1	3412.9	3450.1	607.8	515.9	4832.5	568.1

[1] Miscellaneous and Surpluses

Source:
– SEC (96) 1200-EN, 1996 Edition, Tables 4, 12 and 32
– EC Budgets: 1987, Table 4; 1993 to 1995, Table 5

Table 2 Community expenditure, 1987–1996 (Outturn in payments) (in MECU – current prices)

	1987	1988	1989	1990	1991	1992	1993	1994	1995	1996[1]
1) Community expenditure as % of public expenditure in member states	2.0	2.2	2.0	2.0	2.2	2.2	2.3	2.1	2.1	2.5
2) Expenditure as % of Community GDP	0.96	1.04	0.95	0.95	1.06	1.10	1.20	1.06	1.06	1.24
3) Total Community expenditure, of which	36234.8	42495.2	42284.1	45608.0	55155.8	60300.5	66154.5	61104.4	68138.7	83569.4
a) Structural funds, of which:	5859.6	6419.3	7945.1	9591.4	13971.0	18298.3	20478.5	15872.1	19223.3	26005.6
a1) EAGGF Guidance Section[2]	789.5	1140.9	1349.0	1825.3	2085.4	2847.4	2914.2	2476.5	2530.6	3859.4
a2) ERDF[3]	2560.1	2979.8	3920.0	4554.1	6306.8	8553.8	9545.6	6331.2	8373.6	10663.1
a3) ESF[4]	2510.0	2298.6	2676.1	3212.0	4030.0	4303.7	5382.6	4315.4	4546.9	6031.6
a4) Other[5]	–	–	–	–	–	–	795.0	1246.6	1947.4	2233.3
b) Internal policies, of which:	1327.6	1927.2	2214.3	2691.2	3186.8	3989.0	3587.9	3842.9	3983.3	5545.9
b1) Research and technological development	964.4	1129.5	1517.5	1790.3	1706.3	1903.2	2240.8	2472.2	2544.8	3096.6
b2) Education, vocational training and youth	56.3	86.7	119.8	146.9	219.6	249.1	252.8[1]	263.9[1]	182.6[1]	417.9

Continued. Table 2 Community expenditure, 1987–1996 (Outturn in payments) (in MECU – current prices)

	1987	1988	1989	1990	1991	1992	1993	1994	1995	1996[1]
b3) Other	306.9	711.0	577.0	754.0	1260.9	1836.7	1094.3	1106.8	1255.9	2031.4
c) EAGGF Guarantee Section	22950.1	27635.2	25844.3	27094.2	30960.8	31225.4	34678.4	32906.2	34451.1	42305.0
d) Other	3097.5	6513.5	6280.4	6231.2	7037.2	6787.8	7409.7	8483.2	1048.1	9712.9

(1) Appropriations for payments
(2) EAGGF Guidance Section = European Agricultural Guidance and Guarantee Fund, Guidance Section
(3) ERDF = European Regional Development Fund
(4) ESF = European Social Fund
(5) Cohesion fund, FIFG (Financial Instrument for Fisheries Guidance)

Source:
- SEC (96) 1200 – EN, 1996 Edition, Tables 1 and 3
- Gen.Rep. EC/EU, 1987 (Table 36), 1988 (Table 3), 1989 (Table 2), 1990 (Table 18), 1991 (Table 19), 1992 (Table 23), 1993 (Table 18), 1994 (Table 25) and 1995 (Table 19)
- EC Budgets: 1989 and 1990, ch.63 ; 1991 to 1996, subsection B3, Title B3-1

Table 3 Community expenditure on vocational training through the Structural Funds, 1987–1996 (Outturn in payments) (in MECU – current prices)

	1987	1988	1989	1990	1991	1992	1993	1994	1995	1996[1]
1) Total on Structural Funds, of which:	5859.60	6419.30	7945.10	9591.40	13971.00	18298.30	20478.50	15872.10	19223.30	26005.60
a) European Social Fund (ESF), of which:	2510.00	2298.60	2676.10	3212.00	4030.00	4303.70	5382.60	4315.40	5627.26[1]	6031.60
a1) Objective 1	–	–	2676.10	3211.97	2008.96	2004.40	2626.00	2248.03	3008.87	3127.40
a2) Objective 2	–	–	–	–	313.82	326.93	465.00	339.35	510.78	536.20
a3) Objective 3	–	–	–	–	} 1486.64	1612.66	1828.00	1355.31	1756.75	1851.60
a4) Objective 4	–	–	–	–		–	–	134.56	188.19	332.80
a5) Objective 5(b)	–	–	–	–	58.78	61.15	142.00	67.57	162.67	162.90
a6) Miscellaneous	–	–	–	0.03	161.80	298.56	321.60	170.58	–	20.70
b) Other[2]	3349.60	4120.70	5269.00	6379.4	9941.00	13994.60	15095.90	11556.70	13596.04	19974.00

(1) Appropriations for payments
(2) EAGGF Guidance Section, ERDF, Cohesion Fund, FIFG

Source:
– EC Budgets: 1989 and 1990, ch.60 ; 1991 to 1996, subsection B2, title B2-1

Table 4 Vocational training funding by the ESF by Objective and by Member State, 1989–1994 (Outturn in payments) (in MECU)

	Objective 1 1989–93	Objective 1 1994	Objective 2 1989–93	Objective 2 1994	Objective 3 1989–93[1]	Objective 3 1994	Objective 4 1989–93	Objective 4 1994	Objective 5(b) 1989–93	Objective 5(b) 1994	Total 1989–94
B	–	12.35	69.32	7.93	289.94	64.13	–	2.32	13.00	–	458.99
DK	–	–	11.13	2.35	168.00	35.20	–	0.50	8.00	0.64	225.82
D	853.00[2]	376.22	151.21	51.76	972.43	156.21	–	14.81	49.69	12.87	2638.20
GR	1793.82	444.57	–	–	–	–	–	–	–	–	2238.39
E	2304.66	474.70	284.44	26.76	851.07	125.96	–	27.70	35.05	5.05	4135.39
F	336.62	35.53	271.72	62.47	1645.32	275.12	–	47.70	131.95	32.44	2838.87
IRL	1573.99	339.78	–	–	–	–	–	–	–	–	1913.77
I	1485.42	178.09	127.34	40.67	882.39	128.63	–	30.31	34.23	8.77	2915.85
L	–	–	0.05	1.02	11.21	2.80	–	0.13	–	0.06	15.27
NL	0.07	1.67	63.73	22.78	363.51	136.25	–	11.12	11.68	1.33	612.14
P	2111.40	260.79	–	–	–	–	–	–	–	–	2372.19
UK	318.71	124.33	653.34	123.60	2000.62	431.02	–	–	50.80	6.41	3708.83
Total	10777.69	2248.03	1632.28	339.34	7184.49	1355.32	–	134.59	334.40	67.57	24073.71

[1] Objectives 3 & 4 combined here
[2] Payments to New Lander

Source:
– COM (95) 30 final of 20.3.1995, Annex 1, Tables 1 to 3 and 4
– COM (95) 583 final of 14.12.1995, Table 41 and Annex 1, Tables 1 to 4 and 6

Table 5 Community expenditure on education, vocational training and youth through the educational programmes, 1987–1996 (Outturn in payments) (in MECU – current prices)

	1987	1988	1989	1990	1991	1992	1993[1]	1994[1]	1995[1]	1996[1]
Total on education, vocational training and youth, of which:	56.34	86.79	119.81	146.99	219.62	249.09	252.85	263.90	182.60	417.94
a) Education, of which:	19.71	38.13	62.78	76.02	112.60	121.93	130.45	141.40	84.49	209.43
a1) General education[2]	8.54	8.73	9.29	9.30	13.22	8.98	14.67	17.20	7.92	9.55
a2) Higher education[3]	11.17	28.40	52.49	59.80	73.54	75.89	73.24	80.70	72.68	194.52
a3) Promotion of languages[4]	–	1.00	1.00	6.92	25.84	37.06	42.54	43.50	3.89	5.36
b) Vocational training, of which:	30.87	40.94	45.95	58.60	93.98	115.13	108.14	108.00	76.11	171.75
b1) Initial education and training[5]	0.42	10.84	13.63	12.33	25.72	30.53	34.52	34.50	4.23	1.81
b2) Advanced training[6]	15.28	21.17	23.95	34.23	44.06	56.35	41.46	50.00	59.19	155.32
b3) Continuing training[7]	15.17	8.93	8.37	12.04	24.20	28.25	32.16	23.50	12.69	14.62
c) Youth, of which:	5.76	7.72	11.08	12.37	13.04	12.03	14.26	14.50	22.00	36.76
c1) Young workers and youth measures[8]	5.76	4.98	5.00	5.89	6.10	4.22	4.95	5.00	–	10.00
c2) Youth for Europe	–	2.74	6.08	6.48	6.94	7.81	9.31	9.50	22.00	26.76

Continued. Table 5 Community expenditure on education, vocational training and youth through the educational programmes, 1987–1996 (Outturn in payments) (in MECU – current prices)

(1) Appropriations for payments
(2) Includes Arion, Eurydice
(3) Includes Socrates, Erasmus and Cooperation with third non-European countries
(4) Includes Lingua
(5) Includes Petra
(6) Includes Leonardo, Comett and Eurotecnet
(7) Includes Force
(8) Includes priority measures and other youth exchanges

Source:
– EC Budgets: 1989 and 1990, ch.63 ; 1991 to 1996, Subsection B3, Title B3-1

Table 6 Community expenditure by education and training programme[1], 1987–1996 (Outturn in payments) (in MECU)

	1987	1988	1989	1990	1991	1992	1993[2]	1994[2]	1995[2]	1996[2]	Total
1. COMETT	25.49[3]	21.90	23.96	32.86	41.76	55.12	40.50	33.00	–	–	274.59
2. ERASMUS	11.19	29.98	52.49	59.80	73.54	75.89	73.24	79.70	–	–	455.83
3. PETRA	–	10.85	10.00	8.97	21.16	26.49	30.75	34.50	–	–	142.72
4. YOUTH FOR EUROPE	–	2.74	6.08	6.48	6.94	7.81	9.31	9.50	22.00	26.76	97.62
5. EUROTECNET	–	–	–	1.35	2.30	1.23	0.97	1.00	–	–	6.85
6. LINGUA	–	–	–	5.82	23.84	34.65	39.04	40.00	–	–	143.35
7. FORCE	–	–	–	–	13.85	17.45	20.30	23.50	–	–	75.10
8. EURYDICE/ARION	–	–	–	–	4.83	1.30	1.57	1.50	–	–	9.20
9. LEONARDO	–	–	–	–	–	–	–	–	59.19	155.32	214.51
10. SOCRATES	–	–	–	–	–	–	–	–	70.68	191.51	262.19
SUB-Total (1–10)	36.68	65.47	92.53	115.28	188.22	219.94	215.68	222.70	151.87	373.59	1681.96
11. OTHER ON YOUTH[4]	5.76	4.98	5.00	5.89	6.10	4.22	4.95	5.00	–	10.00	51.90
12. OTHER ON LANGUAGES[5]	–	1.00	1.00	1.10	2.00	2.41	3.50	3.50	3.89	5.36	23.76
13. OTHER ON TRAINING[6]	6.72	9.13	11.99	15.42	14.91	14.84	15.62	16.00	16.92	16.43	137.98
14. OTHER ON EDUCATION[7]	7.18	6.21	9.29	9.30	8.39	7.68	13.10	16.70	9.92	12.56	100.33
Total (1–14)	56.34	86.79	119.81	146.99	219.62	249.09	252.85	263.90	182.60	417.94	1995.93

Continued. Table 6 Community expenditure by education and training programme[1], 1987–1996 (Outturn in payments) (in MECU)

(1) IRIS and TEMPUS do not appear in the EC Budgets
(2) Appropriations for payments
(3) Includes MECU 9.67 for 1986
(4) Includes priority measures and youth exchanges/young workers
(5) Includes less-widespread languages
(6) Includes Cedefop and general measures on vocational training
(7) Includes general education measures and lifelong learning

Source:
– EC Budgets: 1989 and 1990, ch 63; 1991 to 1996, Subsection B3, Title B3-1

Table 7 (a) ERASMUS Programme: Higher education institutions eligible for Erasmus, based on one or more approved Erasmus ICPs

	1988/89	1989/90	1990/91	1991/92	1992/93	1993/94	1994/95
B	26	49	69	76	100	126	142
DK	16	32	44	42	56	60	72
D	83	126	132	176	186	205·	217
GR	12	23	22	24	26	30	32
E	37	42	42	47	55	60	63
F	150	247	268	300	369	405	411
IRL	12	19	20	22	31	31	35
I	43	59	59	65	72	77	85
L	2	2	3	2	2	2	2
NL	24	51	53	72	88	94	96
P	15	28	35	41	67	70	74
UK	106	148	157	172	197	212	220
EUR[1]	–	–	–	–	2	2	1
Total EC	526	826	904	1039	1251	1374	1450
Total EFTA	–	–	–	–	110	176	257
Total	526	826	904	1039	1361	1550	1707

[1] Covers direct allocations to the EPBS ECTS consortium (based in France) and to the European institutions in Arlon and Florence

Source:
– COM (95) 416 final of 8.9.1995, Annex VII

Table 7 (b) ERASMUS Programme: Funds committed for the academic years 1989/90, 1992/93, 1993/94, 1994/95[1] (in 1000 ECU)

	1989/90	1992/93	1993/94	1994/95
1. Action 1, of which	16970.0	22957.0	25343.5	20481.7
1a) ICPs	13920.0	21157.0	23593.5	19086.4
1b) Study visits	3050.0	1800.0	1750.0	1395.3
2. Action 2, of which:	26820.0	62880.1	67880.1	70500.0
2a) Student grants		60000.1	65000.1	67600.0
2b) ECTS student grants		2830.0	2880.0	2900.0
3. Action 3, of which:	1570.0	2040.0	1584.2	2828.7
3a) ECTS institutional grants	840.0	1930.0	1465.0	2761.2
3b) NARIC network grants	730.0	110.0	119.2	67.5
4. Action 4, of which:	7146.0	9316.6	3038.3	2891.7
4a) Publications	489.0	319.8	250.0	187.2
4b) Evaluation and Monitoring	6657.0	8996.8	2788.3	2704.5
5. Total	52506.0	97193.7	97846.1	96702.1

[1] The EU Commission officials were not able or willing to provide additional information for the entire period of the programme

Source:
– COM (95) 416 final of 8.9.1995, Annex I
– COM (94) 281 final of 6.7.1994, Annex I
– COM (93) 268 final of 25.6.1993, Table XV
– COM (90) 128 final of 5.4.1990, Table 7

Table 7 (c) ERASMUS Programme: Allocation of student grant budget (Total Action 2) (in 1000 ECU)

	1988/89	1989/90	1990/91	1991/92	1992/93	1993/94	1994/95
B	392.6	804.6	1240.5	1963.7	2421.6	2665.5	2764.0
DK	213.2	455.9	738.1	899.3	1311.8	1414.0	1239.0
D	2702.7	5578.5	6097.3	8722.0	10894.4	12379.8	12245.0
GR	335.4	697.3	1173.3	1790.1	2220.0	2859.0	2915.0
E	1643.2	3406.1	4343.6	5267.6	6921.6	7389.8	7978.0
F	2226.9	4559.4	5220.8	6561.9	8608.4	9529.5	9978.0
IRL	122.2	268.2	706.1	1037.4	1247.0	1377.2	1498.0
I	2219.1	4613.1	5236.4	6914.1	8820.9	9299.2	9804.0
L	97.5	201.2	210.0	229.1	245.8	249.1	248.0
NL	666.9	1367.8	1839.4	2300.8	3023.7	3133.0	3091.0
P	315.9	643.7	1051.7	1720.5	2437.2	2426.8	2758.0
UK	2064.4	4224.2	4948.8	6410.5	8494.4	8765.9	9366.0
EUR	–	–	74.0	43.0	80.0	85.0	91.0
Total EC	13000.0	26820.0	32880.0	43860.0	56726.8	61573.9	63957.0
Total EFTA	–	–	–	–	6153.2	6306.1	6543.0
Total	13000.0	26820.0	32880.0	43860.0	62880.0	67880.0	70500.0

Source:
– COM (95) 416 final of 8.9.1995, Annex IX
– COM (94) 281 final of 6.7.1994, Annex IX
– COM (93) 268 final of 25.6.1993, Table XII
– COM (90) 128 final of 5.4.1990, p. 8
– EC, Erasmus Department, Table 4.0 (for 1988/89, 1990/91, 1991/92)

Table 7 (d) ERASMUS Programme: Planned student mobility by country (sent/received), 1988/89–1994/95 (Numbers)

	1988/89	1989/90	1990/91*	1991/92*	1992/93	1993/94	1994/95
B	320/330	770/724	1125/1247	1734/1649	4685/4552	5685/5602	6852/6415
DK	120/113	404/279	711/485	736/628	2097/1906	2559/2379	2925/2760
D	2056/1830	3611/2697	4810/3844	6677/4774	11825/11175	15582/14289	18581/17009
GR	164/97	444/230	552/337	848/428	2070/1655	2821/2308	3777/2928
E	1056/970	2131/1923	3356/2984	4268/3869	8661/8420	10930/10720	13784/13464
F	2543/2587	3930/4365	5387/5955	6207/7554	15138/15738	18737/19327	22160/22890
IRL	266/357	340/584	628/948	877/1322	2040/2321	2612/3159	3425/4070
I	700/592	2222/1398	3271/1905	3836/2625	6700/6141	8675/7799	10562/9364
L	–	–	–	–	7/4	10/6	10/7
NL	530/489	1221/996	1920/1477	2478/1990	5777/5514	6897/6925	7992/8040
P	136/128	267/273	529/419	724/620	2273/1831	3010/2401	3654/3064
UK	2348/2851	3472/5334	4921/7601	6451/9376	15438/17732	19284/22767	22286/26949
EUR	–	–	–	–	16/22	30/38	36/44
Total EC	10239	18812	27210	34836	76727/77011	96832/97720	116044/117004
Total EFTA	–	–	–	–	3373/3089	7062/6174	11177/10217
Total	10239	18812	27210	34836	80100	103894	127221

* Also includes Lingua Action II

Source:
– COM (95) 416 final of 8.9.1995, Annex X
– COM (94) 281 final of 6.7.1994, Annex X
– COM (93) 268 final of 25.6.1993, Table X
– COM (89) 119 final of 16.3.1989, Table 7
– EC, Erasmus Department, Table 7.0 (for 1989/90, 1990/91, 1991/92)

Table 8 (a) LINGUA Programme: Community financial support, 1991–1994 (in MECU)

		1991	1992	1993	1994	1991–1994
	Total LINGUA, of which:	23.00	38.00	41.80	44.20	147.00
a	**Action IA**: In-service training of language teachers (individual grants)	4.20	7.30	7.68	8.00	27.18
b	**Action IB**: In-service training of language teachers (European cooperation programmes and preparatory visits)	1.10	1.80	1.98	2.20	7.08
c	**Action II**: Mobility of students and teachers in higher education (ICPs)	4.50	7.60	8.30	8.50	28.90
d	**Action III**: Promoting language learning in the economic world	4.40	7.50	8.14	8.30	28.34
e	**Action IV**: Mobility of young people between the age of 16 and 25 (Joint education projects)	5.70	9.50	10.50	11.50	37.20
f	**Action VA**: Grants for associations, seminars, publications etc	1.10	1.80	1.92	1.90	6.72
g	**Action VB**: Promoting learning of the least widely used, least taught languages of the Community	2.00	2.50	3.28	3.80	11.58

Source:
– COM (95) 458 final of 9.10.1995, p.5
– COM (94) 602 final of 15.12.1994, p.3
– COM (94) 280 final of 6.7.1995, p.6

Table 8 (b) LINGUA Programme: Mobility of participants (students and teachers) in decentralised actions (Action IA and Action IV) and in the "Higher Education" action (Action II) (in numbers)

	1990/91	1991/92	1992/93	1993/94	Total
1. Action IA	516	5257	6037	6802	18612
2. Action II[1]	1897	4180	6724	8847	21648
3. Action IV[2]	4335	19909	25488	33156	82888
Total	6748	29346	38249	48805	123148

[1] The figures here refer to students only
[2] The figures refer to participants, young people and teachers accompanying them (the latter representing 10 per cent of the total on average)

Source:
– COM (95) 458 final of 9.10.1995, pp.19, 21, 36

Table 8 (c) LINGUA Programme: Mobility (sent/received) of foreign language teachers by member state, 1990–1994 (Action IA) (in numbers)

	1990/91	1991/92	1992/93	1993/94	Total
B	18/2	202/21	286/32	265/45	771/100
DK	11/3	98/4	112/2	208/12	429/21
D	137/88	2312/447	1957/581	2236/521	6642/1637
GR	24/5	73/35	169/87	240/79	506/206
E	97/86	460/577	625/588	727/663	1909/1914
F	38/70	480/1416	778/1434	741/1561	2037/4481
IRL	45/7	72/114	101/199	124/435	342/755
I	52/16	613/189	683/283	921/355	2269/843
L	3/0	19/1	7/20	13/5	42/26
NL	18/19	121/29	212/62	217/96	568/206
P	22/7	144/8	243/49	239/51	648/115
UK	51/213	663/2416	864/2700	871/2979	2449/8308
Total	516	5257	6037	6802	18612

Source:
– COM (95) 458 final of 9.10.1995, pp.19–20
– SEC (92) 1073 final of 10.6.1992, Table 1

Table 8 (d) LINGUA Programme: Mobility (sent/received) of young people and teachers accompanying them by member state, 1990–1994 (Action IV) (in numbers)

	1990/91	1991/92	1992/93	1993/94	Total
B	280/160	418/689	665/754	915/843	2278/2446
DK	52/252	830/1130	1124/1170	1415/2399	3421/4951
D	293/520	3140/1777	3120/2418	3503/3137	10056/7852
GR	19/69	304/291	533/627	808/967	1664/1954
E	172/248	2851/1632	5424/1889	6413/2498	14860/6267
F	2583/670	4860/4200	4801/6052	6120/7021	18364/17943
IRL	144/128	455/548	895/662	615/953	2109/2291
I	536/340	2471/1417	3212/2066	7053/3469	13272/7292
L	–	0/42	62/72	172/38	234/152
NL	190/28	1434/418	1708/938	1499/1327	4831/2711
P	81/175	313/280	715/551	1251/1215	2360/2221
UK	800/2560	2833/7485	3229/8289	3392/9289	10254/27623
Total	5150	19909	25488	33156	83703

Source:
– COM (95) 458 final of 9.10.1995, pp.21–22
– SEC (92) 1073 final of 10.6.1992, Tables III & IV

Table 8 (e) LINGUA Programme: Projects accepted and partners in accepted projects in centralised actions, 1991–1994 (in numbers)

	1991		1992		1993		1994		Total	
	Projects	Partners	Projects	Partners	Projects	Partners	Projects	Partners	Projects	Partners
1. Action IB	12	40	25	110	32	130	38	178	107	458
2. Action III	58	195	86	441	97	509	101	566	342	1711
3. Action VA	8	38	14	70	27	105	42	184	91	397
4. Action VB	15	51	23	93	43	191	46	216	127	551
Total	93	324	148	714	199	935	227	1144	667	3117

Source:
– COM (95) 458 final of 9.10.1995, pp.24–25, 28, 31–32

Table 8 (f) LINGUA Programme: Projects accepted in centralised actions by member state, 1992–1994

| | 1992 | | | | | 1993 | | | | | 1994 | | | | | 1992–94 |
	IB	III	VA	VB	Total	IB	III	VA	VB	Total	IB	III	VA	VB	Total	Total
B	2	8	0	1	11	2	6	3	6	17	2	6	4	3	15	43
DK	2	8	0	2	12	2	4	2	2	10	0	4	4	4	12	34
D	2	10	0	4	16	2	18	1	5	26	6	17	2	4	29	71
GR	1	7	0	0	8	1	13	2	3	19	1	12	4	7	24	51
E	1	3	4	0	8	1	7	2	0	10	1	11	6	2	20	38
F	5	15	1	3	24	4	12	9	9	34	6	11	12	7	36	94
IRL	0	2	0	4	6	0	2	1	3	6	0	1	0	4	5	17
I	3	10	1	3	17	3	11	3	4	21	6	11	4	2	23	61
L	1	0	0	0	1	1	1	2	0	4	1	1	1	0	3	8
NL	1	5	2	2	10	2	7	0	5	14	3	6	1	3	13	37
P	1	1	0	3	5	2	3	0	3	8	2	3	0	3	8	21
UK	6	17	6	1	30	12	13	2	3	30	10	18	4	7	39	99
Total	25	86	14	23	148	32	97	27	43	199	38	101	42	46	227	574

Source:
– COM (93) 194 final of 10.5.1993, Annex 5
– COM (94) 280 final of 6.7.1994, Annex 5
– COM (95) 458 final of 9.10.1995, Annex 5

Table 9 (a) TEMPUS Programme (Phare): Overall statistics, 1990–1995

	Tempus I 1990–1993	Tempus II 1994	Tempus II 1995	Total 1990–1995
1 Total Tempus budget (in MECU), of which:	320.81	95.9	102.1	518.81
1a) National indicative programme	272.16	95.9	102.1	470.16
1b) Regional funds	37.75			37.75
1c) Other phare sources	10.90			10.90
2 Joint European Projects (JEPs),	750	464	485	1218
of which new	–	239	229	
3 Joint European Networks (JENs),	–	38	112	121
of which new		38	83	
4 Complementary Measures	138	25	100	263
5 Mobility Flows within JEPs[1]	42784	19550	16641	78658
staff from CEE[2]	15762	7551	6718	30031
staff to CEE	9864	5927	5542	21333
students from CEE	14645	5061	3653	23359
students to CEE	2196	1011	728	3935
6 Individual mobility grands	6864	1369	1271	9504
from CEE	5257	1207	1271	7735
to CEE	1607	162	–	1769

(1) 1994 and 1995 figures are projected figures
(2) CEE = Central and Eastern Europe

Source:
– COM (96) 531 final of 30.10.1996, Annex 1

Table 9 (b) TEMPUS Programme (Phare): Community financial support by country, 1990–1995 (in MECU)

	1990	1991	1992	1993	1994	1995	Total
Total TEMPUS, of which:	23.16	70.50	98.00	129.15	95.90	102.10	518.81
Albania (ALB)	–	–	1.25	4.94	2.40	3.70	12.29
Bulgaria (BG)	–	6.00	8.92	15.71	12.00	12.00	54.63
Czechoslovakia (CS)	3.70	12.80	18.46	–	–	–	34.96
Czech Republic (CZ)	–	–	–	10.94	5.50	8.00	24.44
Slovak Republic (SK)	–	–	–	6.18	5.00	5.00	16.18
Estonia (EE)	–	–	1.01	3.62	1.50	1.50	7.63
Hungary (H)	6.20	16.10	19.27	18.33	16.00	16.00	91.90
Lithuania (LT)	–	–	1.50	5.20	2.00	3.50	12.20
Latvia (LV)	–	–	1.50	4.70	2.00	2.00	10.20
Poland (PL)	12.40	18.10	29.51	37.52	35.00	30.00	162.53
Romania (RO)	–	10.20	13.32	18.23	12.00	18.00	71.75
Slovenia (SLO)	–	–	2.81	3.76	2.50	2.60	11.67
Former Yugoslavia (YU)/DDR	0.90	7.3	–	–	–	–	8.20
Miscellaneous	- 0.04	–	+ 0.45	+ 0.02	–	- 0.20	+ 0.23

Source:
– COM (95) 344 final of 17.7.1995, Annex 2
– COM (96) 531 final of 30.10.1966, Annex 1

Table 9 (c) TEMPUS Programme (Phare): Projects supported by the programme, 1990–1995 (in numbers)

		1990	1991	1992	1993	1994	1995	Total
1	Joint European Projects, of which:	153	452	643	504	464	485	
	1a) Renewed	–	134	403	465	225	256	
	1b) New	153	318	240	39	239	229	1218
2	Joint European Networks	–	–	–	–	38	83	121
3	Complementary Measures	40	37	42	19	25	100	263
4	Youth Activities	65	66	106	114	93	–	444
	Total (1b+2+3+4)	258	421	388	172	395	412	2046

Source:
– COM (95) 344 final of 17.7.1995, Annex 2
– COM (96) 531 final of 30.10.1996, Annex 1

Table 9 (d) TEMPUS Programme (Phare): Joint European Projects by Country, 1990–1995

	1990–1993	1994	1995	Total
Albania	13	17(5)	13(6)	24
Bulgaria	80	59(32)	57(28)	140
Czechoslovakia	145	–	–	145
Czech Republic	81	41(15)	33(14)	110
Slovak Republic	46	33(15)	31(14)	75
Estonia	17	19(13)	12(4)	34
Hungary	204	66(41)	83(38)	283
Lithuania	16	20(5)	18(10)	31
Latvia	17	19(6)	13(5)	28
Poland	248	175(91)	156(65)	404
Romania	94	51(24)	59(36)	154
Slovenia	44	24(5)	12(7)	56
Former Yugoslavia /DDR	70	–	–	70
Total	1075	252	227	1554

Figures in parenthesis represent new projects

Source:
– COM (96) 531 final of 30.10.1996, Annex 2
– COM (95) 344 final of 17.7.1995, Annex 2

Table 9 (e) TEMPUS Programme (Phare): Joint European Projects by Subject area, 1992–1995

	1992 Number	%	1993 Number	%	1994 Number	%	1995 Number	%	Total Number	%
1 Applied Sciences and Technologies	142	60.7	283	56.2	240	51.7	224	46.3	889	52.7
2 Management and Business	40	17.1	80	15.9	78	16.8	88	18.1	286	17.0
3 Natural Sciences and Mathematics	14	6.0	36	7.1	24	5.1	29	6.0	103	6.1
4 Languages and Education/Teacher – Training	21	8.9	56	11.1	19	4.1	19	3.9	115	6.8
5 Social Sciences, Humanities, Art and Design	16	6.9	48	9.5	63	13.7	74	15.2	201	11.9
6 Other	1	0.4	1	0.2	40	8.6	51	10.5	93	5.5
Total	234	100	504	100	464	100	485	100	1687	100

Source:
– COM (96) 531 final of 30.10.1996, Annex 1
– COM (95) 344 final of 17.7.1995, Annex 2
– COM (94) 142 final of 20.4.1994, Annex 2
– COM (93) 30 final of 3.2.1993, Table 2

Table 9 (f) TEMPUS Programme (Phare): Mobility flows within the programme, 1990–1995

	1990	1991	1992	1993	1994	1995	Total
1) Mobility flows within Joint European Projects (new+renewed):							
1a) Staff mobility, of which:	1308	5198	9870	9518	13478	12260	51632
from CEE[1] to EU	724	3148	6014	5876	7551	6718	30031
from EU to CEE	584	2050	3794	3436	5927	5542	21333
from CEE to CEE	–	–	62	206	–	–	268
1b) Student mobility, of which:	1218	3099	6407	6166	6072	4381	27343
from CEE to EU	1033	2747	5612	5253	5061	3653	23359
from EU to CEE	185	352	786	873	1011	728	3935
from CEE to CEE	–	–	9	40	–	–	49
2) Mobility flows on Individual Mobility Grants:							
2a) Staff mobility, of which:	804	986	1396	2239	1369	1271	8065
from EU to CEE	315	280	314	629	162	–	1700
from CEE to EU	489	706	1082	1610	1207	1271	6365
2b) Student mobility, of which:	768	671	–	–	–	–	1439
from EU to CEE	35	34	–	–	–	–	69
from CEE to EU	733	637	–	–	–	–	1370
Total (1a+2a)	2112	6184	11266	11757	14847	13531	59697
Total (1b+2b)	1986	3770	6407	6166	6072	4381	28782

(1) CEE = Central and Eastern Europe

Source:
– COM (96) 531 final of 30.10.1996, Annex 1
– COM (95) 344 final of 17.7.1995, Annex 2

Table 9/1 (a) TEMPUS Programme (Tacis): Overall Statistics, 1993–1995

	Tempus I	Tempus II		
	1993	1994	1995	Total
1. Total Tempus budget (in MECU)	3.45	22.00	22.79	48.24
2. Number of partner states involved	3	7(4)	11(4)	11
3 Number of Pre-JEPs supported	74	76	87	237
4 Number of JEPs supported	–	28	59(31)	59
5 Staff mobility within Pre-JEPs	1421	1174	1304	3899
6 Staff mobility within JEPs	–	586	916	1502
7 Student mobility within JEPs	–	156	95	251
8 Number of partner state universities involved in JEPs				51

Figures in parenthesis represent new states or projects

Source:
– COM (96) 531 final of 30.10.1996, Annex 1

Table 9/1 (b) TEMPUS Programme (Tacis): Allocation of funds and distribution of projects by country, 1993–1995

	Funds (in MECU)				Projects (Pre-JEPs/JEPs)			
	1993	1994	1995	Total	1993	1994	1995	Total
Armenia	–	–	0.247	0.247	–	–	5/0	5/0
Azerbaijan	–	–	0.143	0.143	–	–	4/0	4/0
Belarus	0.380	2.1	1.477	3.957	–	0/4	5/6(2)	5/6
Georgia	–	–	0.242	0.242	–	–	5/0	5/0
Kazakhstan	–	0.370	1.999	2.369	–	9/0	6/3	15/3
Kyrgyzstan	–	0.09	0.754	0.844	–	2/0	2/1	4/1
Moldova	–	0.23	1.128	1.358	–	5/0	4/2	9/2
Mongolia	–	–	0.221	0.221	–	–	5/0	5/0
Russian Federation	2.54	15.37	11.552	29.462	–	0/18	37/34(16)	37/34
Ukraine	0.5	3.32	3.83	7.65	–	0/4	10/9(5)	10/9
Uzbekistan	–	0.25	1.185	1.435	–	6/0	4/2	10/2
Total	3.42	21.73	22.778	47.928	–	22/26	87/57(31)	109/57

Source:
– COM (96) 531 final of 30.10.1996, Annex 3

Table 10 (a) PETRA Programme: Community financial support, 1988–1994 (in MECU)

	1988–1991[1]	1992–1993[1]	1994[2]	1988–1994
Total PETRA, of which:	39.99	64.19	39.00	143.18
a) **Action I**: transnational training and work experience placements	–	30.85	19.80	50.65
b) **Action II**: ENTP (European Network of Training Partnerships) and YIPs (Youth Initiative Projects)	25.68[3]	21.02	12.18	58.88
c) **Action III**: Cooperation in the field of vocational guidance	–	3.00	2.74	5.74
d) Complementary measures	14.31	9.32	4.28	27.91

[1] Actual expenditure
[2] Planned financial support
[3] Includes Actions I & III

Source:
– COM (93) 704 final of 14.1.1994, p.15

Table 10 (b) PETRA Programme: Staff and young people involved in the activities of the programme, 1988–1994 (in numbers)

	1988–1991	1992–1994	1988–1994
1. Staff (teachers, trainers, tutors)	10000	20000	30000
2. Young people, of which:	60000	140000	200000
2a) Action I	}	40000	40000
2b) Action II	} 60000	100000	160000
3. Projects in the Network (ENTP)	488	330	818
4. Projects in YIPs	575	225	800

The figures approximate the exact numbers

Source:
– COM (93) 48 final of 11.2.1993, pp.28–29, 33
– COM (93) 403 final of 14.1.1994, pp.10–11

Table 11 (a) COMETT – I Programme: Amounts allocated by strand and year, 1987–1989 (in 1000 ECU)

Strand	1987 (R1)	1987 (R2)	1988 (R3)	1988 (Ren)	1989 (R4)	1989 (Ren)	1987–1989
A	2783	725	665	406	–	4457	9036
Ba	937	1755	1211	–	931	–	4834
BaP	–	–	2063	–	4835	–	6898
Bb	102	337	466	–	602	–	1507
C	1835	2602	2584	3907	–	5774	16702
D	1295	131	138	2485	–	3523	7572
Miscellaneous	–	1800	–	1800	–	2351	5951
Total	6952	7350	7127	8598	6368	16105	52500

R1, R2, R3, R4 = successive application rounds
Ren = projects accepted for renewal
Strand A = University-Enterprises Training Partnerships ('UETPs')
Strand Ba-BaP = Transnational student placements in enterprises
Strand Bb = Transnational fellowships
Strand C = Joint continuing training projects
Strand D = Multilateral multimedia training initiatives

Source:
– COM (90) 119 final of 11.4.1990, Table 5

Table 11 (b) COMETT-I Programme: Distribution of projects accepted by strand and year, 1987–1989

Strand	1987 (R1)	1987 (R2)	1988 (R3)	1989 (R4)	Total
A	79	28	19	-0-	126
Ba	80	145	171	161	557
BaP	-0-	-0-	67	89	156
Bb	14	48	71	88	221
C	57	80	97	-0-	234
D	27	30	32	-0-	89
Total	257	331	457	338	1383

Data displayed are the number of **new** projects accepted during successive application rounds

Source:
– COM (90) 119 final of 11.4.1990, Table 3

Table 11 (c) COMETT-I Programme: Distribution of projects accepted by strand and applicant member state, 1987–1989

	A	Ba	BaP	Bb	C	D	Total
B	7	30	6	15	25	7	90
DK	4	18	2	2	7	2	35
D	11	61	16	12	20	6	126
GR	8	25	4	40	22	5	104
E	15	38	22	30	10	7	122
F	23	176	37	39	57	27	359
IRL	3	22	6	10	7	2	50
I	16	18	13	20	24	8	99
L	1	–	–	–	–	–	1
NL	6	45	6	7	16	3	83
P	11	21	10	15	10	2	69
UK	21	91	34	26	15	19	206
Total	126	545	156	216	213	88	1344

Source:
– COM (90) 119 final of 11.4.1990, Table 4

Table 11 (d) COMETT -II Programme: Allocations and mobility, 1990–1994

| | Allocations (in 1000 ECU) | | | | | | Mobility: 1990–1994 | |
	1990	1991	1992	1993	1994	1990–1994	Students[1]	Fellows[2]
B	4374	898	1895	926	1085	9178	1030	45
DK	2843	742	1341	718	761	6405	909	24
D	10228	2498	7421	3851	4035	28033	4447	48
GR	5478	1271	3031	1861	1862	13503	1957	77
E	6188	1932	4325	2379	2497	17321	2595	82
F	13743	3250	7681	4383	4389	33446	5831	71
IRL	3633	1136	2280	1016	1213	9278	1205	46
I	8414	1874	4746	2671	2717	20422	2867	83
L	1035	–	150	–	170	1355	50	–
NL	5490	1058	2765	1435	1487	12235	1567	15
P	3344	962	2063	1196	1515	9080	1321	59
UK	12826	3748	7976	4294	4162	33006	4785	69
Total EC	77596	19369	45674	24730	25893	193262	28564	619
Total EFTA[3]	7448	2278	10991	4062	3827	28606	3091	220
Total	85044	21647	56665	28792	29720	221.868	31.655	839

(1) Transnational student placements in enterprises (Strand Ba+ Bb)
(2) Exchanges of staff between higher education and industry
(3) Austria, Norway, Sweden, Finland, Ireland, Switzerland, Liechtenstein

Source:
– COM (96) 410 final of 16.9.1996, Annex 1, Table 7; and Annex 2

Table 11 (e) COMETT-II Programme: Distribution of allocations by strand and year, 1990–1994 (in 1000 ECU)

Strand	1990	1991	1992	1993	1994	Total
A	21605	–	7607	–	–	29212
Ba	10148	14279	17708	18491	18954	79580
Bb	99	–	–	–	–	99
Bc	613	907	946	1680	1762	5908
Ca	2123	6212	7119	5161	6282	26897
Cb	35591	–	23288	–	–	58879
Cc	14770	–	–	–	–	14770
D	95	248	–	3461	2722	6526
Total	85044	21646	56668	28793	29720	221871

Strand A = University – Enterprises Training Partnerships ('UETPs')
Strand Ba = Transnational student placements in enterprises
Strand Bb = Transnational long graduate placements
Strand Bc = Exchanges of staff between higher education and industry
Strand Ca = Advanced short courses
Strand Cb = Joint training projects (development of courses and training materials)
Strand Cc = Training projects with emphasis on structural impact ('Pilot Projects')
Strand D = Complementary measures (studies, reports, conferences etc)

Source:
– COM (96) 410 final of 16.9.1996, Table 5

Table 11 (f) COMETT – II Programme: Distribution of allocations by country and strand, 1990–1994 (in 1000 ECU)

	A	Ba/Bb/Bc	Ca	Cb/Cc	D	Total
B	1035	2817	1410	3745	172	9179
DK	675	2315	595	2645	174	6404
D	3937	11504	3089	8719	784	28033
GR	1890	5621	1603	4089	300	13503
E	2505	7510	2088	4633	584	17320
F	4265	13083	3995	10968	1134	33445
IRL	690	3605	1262	3518	204	9279
I	2753	7496	2575	7015	583	20422
L	120	105	45	1065	20	1355
NL	1455	3804	1685	4963	328	12235
P	1350	3687	1195	2470	379	9081
UK	3860	14036	3347	10679	1087	33009
Total EC	24535	75583	22889	64509	5749	193265
Total EFTA	4677		10003	9140	779	24599
Total	29212	75583	32892	73649	6528	217864

Source:
– COM (96) 410 final of 16.9.1996, Table 8

Table 11 (g) COMETT-II Programme: Distribution of projects accepted by strand and year, 1990–1994

Strand	1990	1991	1992	1993	1994	Total
A	158	–	49	–	–	207
Ba	246	148	172	177	175	918
Bb	13	–	–	–	–	13
Bc	66	54	67	86	92	365
Ca	123	130	154	188	179	774
Cb	191	–	113	–	–	304
Cc	30	–	–	–	–	30
D	49	88	–	146	141	424
Total	876	420	555	597	587	3035

Source:
– COM (96) 410 final of 16.9.1996, Table 2

Table 11 (h) COMETT-II Programme: Distribution of projects accepted by country and year, 1990–1994

	1990	1991	1992	1993	1994	Total
B	49	17	19	16	15	116
DK	24	11	12	15	14	76
D	88	43	77	76	71	355
GR	63	25	29	34	31	182
E	61	30	47	55	57	250
F	166	63	80	91	88	488
IRL	47	16	18	18	17	116
I	76	37	48	63	61	285
L	4	–	1	–	3	8
NL	49	21	23	24	22	139
P	38	25	30	34	34	161
UK	128	61	71	78	84	422
Total EC	793	349	455	504	497	2598
Total EFTA	84	52	100	93	92	421
Total	877	401	555	597	589	3019

Source:
– COM (96) 410 final of 16.9.1996, Table 6

Table 12   EUROTECNET Programme: Operations of the Programme, 1990–1992

	1990	1991	1992	Total
1) Budget allocations (ECU)	1952000	2311000	2851000	7114000
2) Budget execution (ECU)	1764000	2311000	2851000	6926000
3) Projects and Actions	• Exchange of information on 277 innovative training projects initiated by member states • Dissemination of results through more than 100 specialised seminars annually			
4) Mobility and Exchange	• Bilateral and multitateral exchanges of scientific specialists (350–400 persons annually) between EUROTECNET projects			

Source:
– COM (93) 151 final of 5.5.1993, Tables 1–4
– COM (93) 317 final of 14.7.1993, p.46

Table 13 (a)   FORCE   Programme: Community   financial   support, 1991–1993 (in MECU)

	1991	1992	1993	Total
Total FORCE, of which:	14.0	19.4	24.0	57.4
a) **Action I**: Support for innovation in continuing vocational training (refers to direct projects)	9.5	13.3	17.9	40.7
b) **Action II**: analysis, monitoring, assessment and forecasting (refers to research projects: sectoral surveys, analysis of contractual policy, statistical survey)	1.1	2.0	2.5	5.6
c) **Action III**: accompanying measures (technical assistance, evaluation, information)	3.4	4.1	3.6	11.1

Source:
– COM (94) 418 final of 13.10.1994, p.10

Table 13 (b) FORCE Programme: Overall distribution of FORCE projects and initial amount allocated according to the country of origin of the contractor, 1991–93

Country	No Projects	Initial amount allocated (ECU)
B	58	5039000
DK	31	2720000
D	76	6698500
GR	72	5490500
E	84	6649600
F	89	6544375
IRL	48	3516000
I	79	6727000
L	12	1026500
NL	36	2730000
P	44	3421475
UK	91	7380400
Total	720	57943350

Source:
– COM (94) 418 final of 13.10.1994, p.17

Table 13 (c) FORCE Programme: Overall view of participation in the FORCE projects by type of organisation, 1991–93

	Contractors[1]	Partners
1) Enterprises or groups of enterprises	260	2979
2) Employers' organisations	60	335
3) Trade Union organisations	53	462
4) Joint bodies	31	58
5) Training organisations	170	928
6) Chambers of Commerce	17	105
7) Public authorities	4	83
8) Other (including universities, training consortia, etc)	125	862
Total	720	5812

[1] The number of contractors is equal to the number of projects

Source:
– COM (94) 418 final of 13.10.1994, pp.16–17

Table 14 (a) YOUTH FOR EUROPE Programme: Community financial support, 1988–1994 (in 1000 ECU)

	1988–1991	1992	1993	1994	1988–1994
Total YOUTH FOR EUROPE, of which	22200.0	10000.0	9500.0	16280.0	57980.0
a) **Action I.1**: direct grants to young people	15940.0	7180.0	7280.0	11700.0	42100.0
b) **Action I.2**: voluntary service	260.0	120.0	120.0	195.0	695.0
c) **Action I.3**: study visits	800.0	360.0	360.0	585.0	2105.0
d) **Action I.4, I.5**: professional development for youth workers and pilot projects	755.0	340.0	340.0	550.0	1985.0
e) **Action II**: European level activities and technical support	2225.0	1000.0	500.0	1500.0	5225.0
f) National agencies	2220.0	1000.0	900.0	1750.0	5870.0

Source:
– COM (95) 159 final of 11.5.1995, Annex 1
– COM (93) 524 final of 28.10.1993, Annex 1
– COM (93) 151 final of 5.5.1993 (calculations)
– EC, 1996 Budget, p.884 (outturn payments)

Table 14 (b) YOUTH FOR EUROPE Programme: Financial aid for youth exchanges by member state, 1988–1993 (Action I.1). (in MECU)

	1988–1991	1992	1993	1988–1993
B	0.83	0.27	0.27	1.37
DK	0.67	0.22	0.23	1.12
D	3.38	1.10	1.10	5.58
GR	1.01	0.33	0.34	1.68
E	2.50	0.81	0.83	4.14
F	2.52	0.82	0.82	4.16
IRL	0.64	0.21	0.22	1.07
I	3.04	0.99	1.00	5.03
L	0.46	0.15	0.15	0.76
NL	1.07	0.35	0.36	1.78
P	1.04	0.34	0.35	1.73
UK	2.76	0.90	0.90	4.56
EC	2.18	0.71	0.73	3.62
Total	22.10	7.20	7.30	36.60

Source:
– COM (95) 159 final of 11.5.1995, Annex 1
– COM (93) 524 final of 28.10.1993, Annex 1
– EC, 1994, p.30

Table 14 (c) YOUTH FOR EUROPE Programme: Breakdown of age of participants for 1992 (Action I.1.)

Age	Participants (%)
15–17	22
18–19	24
20–22	28
23–25	21
25+	5

Source:
– COM (93) 524 final of 28.10.1993, p.12

Table 15 (a) EXCHANGE OF YOUNG WORKERS: Participants and Community financial support, 1985–1991 (Third Joint Project)

	1985	1986	1987	1988	1989	1990	1991	1985–1991
Participants (in numbers)	1309	3109	2304	2676	2768	2644	2567	17377
Financial support (in MECU)	2.0	4.5	4.5	4.5	5.0	5.5	6.0	32.0

Source:
– COM (92) 512 final of 7.12.1992, p.14

Table 15 (b) EXCHANGE OF YOUNG WORKERS: Flow (sent/received) of participants by member state, 1985–1991 (Third Joint Project)

	1985	1986	1987	1988	1989	1990	1991	1985–1991
B	35/38	102/120	77/81	77/51	89/93	102/145	77/140	559/668
DK	113/67	224/243	234/206	135/176	223/143	169/234	176/133	1274/1202
D	171/260	344/362	292/325	295/276	324/386	386/316	336/244	2148/2169
GR	42/35	80/54	182/124	189/114	198/134	183/127	133/57	1007/645
E	0/0	136/94	259/142	206/158	231/221	235/142	257/231	1324/988
F	359/240	685/638	600/685	499/528	553/548	596/572	620/720	3912/3931
IRL	142/167	306/292	290/220	230/223	279/233	200/252	194/188	1641/1575
I	170/116	482/489	485/553	382/498	379/404	242/224	214/200	2354/2484
L	11/0	9/15	16/15	7/3	7/4	15/2	10/5	75/44
NL	98/100	248/261	317/224	283/191	242/270	215/220	199/205	1602/1471
P	0/0	94/45	179/238	202/183	222/208	216/209	154/194	1067/1077
UK	168/286	399/496	430/548	301/405	297/400	414/530	437/490	2446/3155
Total	1309	3109	3361	2806	3044	2973	2807	19409

Source:
– COM (92) 512 final of 7.12.1992, Annex 5

Table 16   MIGRANTS' CHILDREN: Foreign pupils in % of total school population in the EU, 1975–1990

Member State	Pre-primary Education				Primary Education				Secondary Education			
	1975/76	1980/81	1985/86	1989/90	1975/76	1980/81	1985/86	1989/90	1975/76	1980/81	1985/86	1989/90
B	10.0[1]	13.0	11.6	10.4	10.2	12.9	12.0	11.2	7.5[1]	9.2	7.8	8.0
DK	–	–	–	–	–	–	–	–	n.a	1.2	1.4	3.5
D	n.a	n.a	n.a	n.a	included in secondary figures				3.7	6.4	7.8	10.2
F	7.4	9.1	9.6	8.8	7.4	8.9	10.6	10.1	4.9	5.6	6.6	7.0
I	n.a	n.a	0.1	0.2	n.a	n.a	0.1	0.2	n.a	n.a	0.1	0.1
L	31.0[1]	41.5[2]	–	28.8	28.2[1]	38.3[2]	36.1	32.0	–	–	–	–
NL	–	–	–	–	1.6	4.2[3]	5.7[3]	7.0[3]	n.a.	1.9	3.0	3.8

(1) 1974/75
(2) 1981/82
(3) includes pre-primary

Source:
– COM (94) 80 final of 25.3.1994, Appendix 2

Table 17 Breakdown of resident population in the EU (at 1 January 1992)

	Non-Community foreigners		Community foreigners		Nationals	
	(1000)	(%)	(1000)	(%)	(1000)	(%)
B	316	3.6	559	5.6	9099	90.8
DK	130	2.5	39	0.8	4993	96.7
D	4184	5.2	1699	2.1	74208	92.7
GR	146	1.4	68	0.7	10066	97.9
E	194	0.5	167	0.4	38695	99.1
F	2275	4.0	1322	2.3	53055	93.7
IRL	22	0.6	73	2.1	3454	97.3
I	418	0.7	119	0.2	56220	99.1
L	13	3.2	116	28.9	272	67.9
NL	551	3.6	182	1.2	14396	95.2
A	438	5.6	79	1.0	7278	93.4
P	83	0.8	31	0.3	9741	98.8
FIN	26	0.5	12	0.2	4991	99.3
S	346	4.0	148	1.7	8150	94.3
UK	1194	2.1	818	1.4	54948	96.5
Total EU	10336	2.9	5432	1.4	349566	95.7

Source:
– Eurostat, Europe in Figures, 4th Edition, 1995, p.155

Table 18 GDP[1] per capita in PPS[2], 1985–1995 (EUR 15=100)

	1985	1986	1987	1988	1989	1990	1991	1992	1993	1994	1995
B	104	102	102	102	103	103	107	110	113	113	112
DK	113	114	111	109	106	105	109	106	112	114	114
D	118	117	116	115	115	116	106	109	108	110	110
GR	62	61	59	59	60	57	60	61	63	63	63
E	70	70	72	73	74	74	80	78	78	76	76
F	111	110	109	110	110	110	114	112	109	108	107
IRL	63	63	65	65	67	71	75	78	80	85	90
I	102	102	102	102	102	101	105	105	102	103	103
L	139	144	140	143	147	144	152	153	163	162	165
NL	103	103	101	99	100	101	103	103	104	104	104
A	107	105	104	104	104	105	108	109	112	113	112
P	46	54	55	56	58	59	63	64	67	67	67
FIN	102	101	102	103	105	103	94	87	92	91	92
S	114	113	113	111	110	108	105	100	99	98	98
UK	100	102	103	104	103	101	98	98	100	99	99
EUR15	100	100	100	100	100	100	100	100	100	100	100

[1] GDP = Gross Domestic Product
[2] PPS = Parchasing Power Standard

Source:
– Eurostat, *Statistics in Focus: Economy and Finance,* No 5, 1996, Table 4

Table 19 (a) JEAN MONNET Project: Academic initiatives by subject and country, 1990–1996

	Jean Monnet Chairs					Permanent Courses					European Modules					Research Projects					Compl. Initiatives					Total
	a	b	c	d	e	a	b	c	d	e	a	b	c	d	e	a	b	c	d	e	a	b	c	d	e	
B	3	2	1	1	–	8	8	4	3	–	4	10	1	1	5	2	–	–	1	–	1	–	–	–	–	55
DK	1	3	4	1	–	–	3	3	3	3	–	–	4	2	–	1	1	1	–	–	–	1	–	–	–	31
D	12	10	8	8	–	9	15	20	5	8	8	10	8	1	8	1	2	2	2	1	2	1	–	–	–	141
GR	4	4	3	–	–	10	12	10	2	4	2	14	4	1	–	1	1	2	–	–	–	–	–	–	–	74
E	21	14	6	6	–	31	15	3	3	3	9	8	1	1	4	–	6	–	–	–	4	4	–	–	–	139
F	25	13	1	3	–	45	28	11	12	9	13	18	7	3	25	10	2	–	–	–	4	3	–	1	–	233
IRL	3	3	8	2	–	1	4	2	–	–	–	2	4	–	1	–	1	–	–	–	1	–	–	1	2	36
I	17	6	3	5	–	38	14	4	4	10	21	24	10	9	14	2	3	1	2	3	2	–	1	1	–	193
L	–	–	–	–	–	–	–	–	1	–	–	–	–	–	–	–	–	–	–	–	–	–	–	–	–	1
NL	7	7	1	2	–	17	4	11	4	7	4	2	4	1	5	2	–	–	–	–	–	1	–	–	–	79
A	3	1	–	–	–	–	–	–	1	–	–	–	–	1	2	1	1	–	–	–	–	–	–	–	–	10
P	3	4	2	–	–	8	9	2	–	2	4	10	1	–	4	1	–	1	–	–	–	–	1	–	–	52
FIN	1	1	2	–	–	3	–	–	1	1	1	2	2	–	2	–	–	1	–	–	–	–	–	–	–	17
S	2	1	1	–	–	3	1	1	1	1	1	–	2	–	–	–	–	–	–	–	–	–	–	–	–	13
UK	19	14	33	3	–	11	20	26	7	10	10	17	23	5	19	2	3	8	–	–	3	1	2	–	–	236
Total	121	82	73	31	–	184	133	97	47	58	77	117	71	25	89	23	20	16	5	5	17	11	3	3	2	1310

a = EC Law
b = Economics
c = Political Science
d = History
e = Multidisciplinary

Source:
– *European University News*, no.194, June 1996, p.21

Table 19 (b) JEAN MONNET Project: Academic initiatives in Hungary and Poland, 1996/1997

	(1) Hungary							(2) Poland							Total 1+2
	a	b	c	d	e	f	Total	a	b	c	d	e	f	Total	
Jean Monnet Chairs	1	3	1	–	–	–	5	1	1	–	–	–	–	2	7
Permanent Courses	2	1	3	1	–	–	7	4	6	5	2	2	1	20	27
European Modules	–	2	1	–	–	–	3	–	1	2	–	1	–	4	7
Research Projects	–	1	–	–	–	–	1	–	1	–	–	–	–	1	2
Doctoral Grants	–	–	–	–	–	–	–	–	1	1	–	–	–	2	2
Teaching Materials	2	2	4	1	–	–	9	4	4	3	2	1	–	14	23
Complementary	2	1	–	–	–	–	3	–	–	–	–	–	–	–	3
Total	7	10	9	2	–	–	28	9	14	11	4	4	1	43	71

a = EC Law
b = Economics
c = Political Science
d = History
e = Multidisciplinary
f = Other

Source:
– *European University News,* No 195, September 1996, p.28

Table 20 EU Education and Training Programmes

Short title	Full Title	Duration	EU Funding (MECU) up to 1996
COMETT	Programme on cooperation between universities and industry regarding training in the field of technology	1986–1989 1990–1994	274.59
ERASMUS	European Community action scheme for the mobility of university students	1987–1990 1991–1994 1995–1996	455.83
PETRA	Action programme for the vocational training of young people and their preparation for adult and working life	1988–1991 1992–1994	142.72
YOUTH FOR EUROPE	Action programme for the promotion of youth exchanges in the Community	1988–1991 1992–1994 1995–1999	97.62
IRIS	European network of vocational training projects for women	1988–1993	0.75
EURO- TECNET	Action programme to promote innovation in the field of vocational training resulting from technological change in the European Community	1989–1994	6.85
LINGUA	Action programme to promote foreign language competence in the European Community	1990–1994 1995–1996	143.35
TEMPUS	Trans-European mobility scheme for university studies	1990–1993 1994–1998	518.81
FORCE	Action programme for the development of continuing vocational training in the European Community	1991–1994	75.10
LEONARDO	Action programme for the implementation of a European Community vocational training policy	1995–1999	214.51
SOCRATES	European Community action programme on education	1995–1999	262.19
JEAN MONNET PROJECT	Action programme for the development of European integration in universities through the creation and development of courses	1990–	16.88

Bibliography

(a) EU Publications

Commission of the EC, *Key data on education in the European Union 1995,* Luxembourg: Office for Official Publications of the European Communities, 1996

Commission of the EC, *Structures of the Education and Initial Training Systems of the European Union,* Luxembourg: Office for Official Publications of the European Communities, 1995

Commission of the EC, 'Intergovernmental Conferences: Contributions by the Commission', *Bulletin of the European Communities,* Supplement 2/91

Commission of the EC, 'For a Community policy on education' (Henri Janne Report), *Bulletin of the European Communities,* Supplement 10/1973

Commission of the EC, 'Commission communication on education in the European Community', *Bulletin of the European Communities,* Supplement 3/74

Commission of the EC, 'A People's Europe: Reports from the ad hoc Committee' (Adonnino Report), *Bulletin of the European Communities,* Supplement 7/85

COM(78)222 final: Commission proposal for an action programme on the teaching of languages in the Community, 14 June 1978

COM(83)482 final: Commission proposal for a Council Decision on the comparability of vocational training qualifications between the member states of the Community, 7 September 1983

COM(84)54 final: Commission report on the implementation of Directive 77/486/EEC on the education of the children of migrant workers, 10 February 1984

COM(84)446 final: Commission proposal on 'A people's Europe-Implementing the conclusions of the Fontainebleau European Council', 24 September 1984

COM(84)722 final: Commission communication on the new information technologies and the school systems in the European Community, 14 December 1984

COM(85)355 final: Commission proposal on a general system for the recognition of higher education diplomas, 22 July 1985 (See also the same document in Commission of the EC, "A general system for the recognition of higher education diplomas", *Bull. of the EC,* Supplement 8/85)

COM(85)767 final: Commission report on the transition of young people from education to adult and working life, 23 December 1985

COM(86)780 final: Commission communication on adult training in firms, 23 January 1987

COM(87)705 final: Commission report on the transition of young people from education to adult and working life, 23 December 1987

COM(88)36 final: Commission report on the Comett programme: 1987 activities report, 12 February 1988

COM(88)203 final: Commission communication on the teaching of foreign languages, 18 April 1988

COM(88)280 final: Commission communication entitled 'Education in the European Community: Medium-term perspectives, 1989–92', 18 May 1988

COM(88)787 final: Commission report on the implementation of Directive 77/486/EEC on the education of the children of migrant workers, 3 January 1989

COM(88)841 final: Commission proposals on teaching and learning of foreign languages (establishing the Lingua programme), 6 January 1989

COM(89)119 final: Commission report on the Erasmus programme: 1988 annual report, 16 March 1989

COM(89)171 final: Commission report on the Comett programme: Report of 1988 activities, 13 April 1989

COM(89)236 final: Commission communication entitled 'Education and training in the European Community: Guidelines for the medium term 2 June 1989

COM(89)567 final: Commission communication proposing the adoption of a Community action programme on the development of continuing vocational training (Force), 8 December 1989

COM(90)119 final: Commission report on the Comett programme: Report of 1989 activities, 11 April 1990

COM(90)128 final: Commission report on the Erasmus programme: 1989 annual report, 5 April 1990

COM(90)377 final: Commission report on the Third Joint Programme for the exchange of young workers, 1988–1989, 1 August 1990

COM(90)378 final: Commission report on the 'Youth for Europe' programme: 1988/89 annual report, 1 August 1990

COM(91)349 final: Commission memorandum on 'higher education in the European Community', 5 November 1991

COM(91)355 final: Commission report on the 'Youth for Europe' programme: 1990 annual report, 4 October 1991

COM(91)388 final: Commission memorandum on open distance learning in the European Community, 12 November 1991

COM(91)397 final: Commission memorandum on vocational training in the European Community in the 1990s, 12 December 1991

COM(92)457 final: Commission communication concerning European higher education-industry cooperation: Advanced training for competitive advantage, 9 December 1992

COM(92)512 final: Commission report on the Third Joint Programme for the exchange of young workers, 1985–1991, 7 December 1992

COM(93)30 final: Commission report on the Tempus programme: 1991/92 annual report, 3 February 1993

COM(93)48 final: Commission report on the implementation of the Petra programme (1988–1991), 11 February 1993

COM(93)151 final: Commission report on EC education and training programmes, 1986–1992: Results and achievements, an overview, 5 May 1993

COM(93)183 final: Commission Working Paper entitled 'Guidelines for Community action in the field of education and training', 5 May 1993

COM(93)194 final: Commission report on the Lingua programme: 1992 activity report, 10 May 1993

COM(93)268 final: Commission report on the Erasmus programme: 1992 annual report, 25 June 1993

COM(93)317 final: Commission report on the operation of the Eurotecnet programme, 1990/92, 14 July 1993

COM(93)457 final: Commission Green Paper on 'the European dimension of education', 29 September 1993

COM(93)521 final: Commission report on priority actions in the youth field: 1992 activity report, 28 October 1993

COM(93)524 final: Commission report on the 'Youth for Europe' programme: 1992 annual report, 28 October 1993

COM(93)700 final: Commission White Paper on 'Growth, competitiveness, employment: The challenges and ways forward into the 21st century', 5 December 1993 (for education and training see ch.7: 'Adaptation of education and vocational training systems')

COM(93)704 final: Commission report on the implementation of the PETRA programme, 14 January 1994

COM(94)80 final: Commission report on the education of migrants' children in the European Union, 22 March 1994

COM(94) 142 final: Commission report on the Tempus programme: 1992/93 annual report, 20 April 1994

COM(94)280 final: Commission report on the Lingua programme: 1993 activity report, 6 July 1994

COM(94)281 final: Commission report on the Erasmus programme: 1993 annual report, 6 July 1994

COM(94)333 final: Commission White Paper entitled "European Social Policy: A Way Forward for the Union", 27 July 1994

COM(94)418 final: Commission interim report on the Force programme, 13 October 1994

COM(94)528 final: Commission communication on the education and training in the face of technological, industrial and social challenges, 23 November 1994

COM(94)533 final: Commission report on the application of the subsidiarity principle (1994), 25 November 1994

COM(94)596 final: Commission communication on recognition of qualifications for academic and professional purposes, 13 December 1994

COM(94)602 final: Report of activities (1989–93) concerning the lesser used languages of the European Union, 15 December 1994

COM(95)30 final: Commission report on the Structural Funds: fifth annual report for 1993, 20 March 1995

COM(95)90 final: Commission report on priority actions in the youth field: 1993 activity report, 27 March 1995

COM(95)159 final: Commission report on the 'Youth for Europe' programme: 1993 annual report, 11 May 1995

COM(95)344 final: Commission report on the Tempus programme: 1993/94 annual report, 17 July 1995

COM(95)388 final: Commission report on the European Training Foundation: 1994 annual report, 21 September 1995

COM(95)416 final: Commission report on the Erasmus programme: 1994 annual report, 8 September 1995

COM(95)458 final: Commission report on the Lingua programme: 1994 activity report, 9 October 1995

COM(95)583 final: Commission report on the Structural Funds: sixth annual report for 1994, 14 December 1995

COM(95)590 final: Commission White Paper on education and training entitled 'Teaching and Learning: Towards the Learning Society', 29 November 1995

COM(96)46 final: Commission report on the state of application of the general system for the recognition of higher education diplomas, 15 February 1996

COM(96)360 final: Commission report on the Phare Programme: Annual Report 1995, 23 July 1996

COM(96)410 final: Commission report on Comett-II: The final evaluation report, 16 September 1996

COM(96)428 final: Commission report on the evaluation of the first phase of Tempus, 1990/91–1993/94, 20 September 1996

COM(96)462 final: Commission Green Paper on 'Education, training, research: The obstacles to transnational mobility', published in *Bulletin of the European Union*, Supplement 5/96

COM(96)471 final: Commission communication on 'Learning in the information society: Action plan for a European education initiative, 1996–98', 2 October 1996

COM(96)485: European Commission, 'Employment in Europe, 1996'

COM(96)502 final: 7th annual report on the Structural Funds, 1995, 30 October 1996

COM(96)531 final: Commission report on the Tempus programme: annual report (1.8.1994–31.12.1995), 30 October 1996

COM(96)600 final: Thirteenth annual report on monitoring the application of Community law (1995), 29 May 1996

Council of the EC, *European Education Policy Statements*, second edition, Luxembourg: Office for Official Publications of the EC, 1986

Council of the EC, *European Education Policy Statements*, Supplement no.2 to the third edition, Luxembourg: Office for Official Publications of the EC, 1993

EC, Commission report on the 'Lingua Programme', Activity Report 1991, 10 June 1992 [SEC(92)1073 final]

EC, "Cooperation in Education in the European Union, 1976–1994", *Studies No5*, Luxembourg: Office for Official Publications of the European Communities, 1994

EC, *Basic Statistics of the European Union: Comparisons with the principal partners of the Union*, 32nd edition, Luxembourg: Office for Official Publications of the European Communities, 1995

EC, *The Community Budget: The Facts in Figures*, Luxembourg: Office for Official Publications of the European Communities, 1996 [SEC(96)1200-EN]

European Parliament 87/186/ECSC, EEC, Euratom: Final adoption of the general budget of the European Communities for the year 1987: OJ L86, 30 March 1987

European Parliament 88/421/ECSC, EEC, Euratom: Final adoption of the general budget of the European Communities for the year 1988: OJ L226, 16 August1988

European Parliament 89/40/ECSC, EEC, Euratom: Final adoption of the general budget of the European Communities for the year 1989: OJ L26, 30 January 1989

European Parliament 90/26/ECSC, EEC, Euratom: Final adoption of the general budget of the European Communities for the year 1990: OJ L24, 29 January 1990

European Parliament 91/34/ECSC, EEC, Euratom: Final adoption of the general budget of the European Communities for the year 1991: OJ L30, 4 February 1991

European Parliament 92/41/ECSC, EEC, Euratom: Final adoption of the general budget of the European Communities for the year 1992: OJ L26, 3 February 1992

European Parliament 93/62/ECSC, EEC, Euratom: Final adoption of the general budget of the European Communities for the year 1993: OJ L31, 8 February 1993

European Parliament 94/56/ECSC, EEC, Euratom: Final adoption of the general budget of the European Communities for the year 1994: OJ L34, 7 February 1994

European Parliament 95/474/ECSC, EEC, Euratom: Final adoption of the general
    budget of the European Communities for the year 1995: OJ L276, 20 November
    1995
European Parliament 96/96/ECSC, EEC, Euratom: Final adoption of the general
    budget of the European Communities for the year 1996: OJ L22, 29 January 1996
Eurostat, *Europe in Figures*, 4th edition, Luxembourg: Office for Official Publications of
    the European Communities, 1995

(b) Articles and Books

Althusser, L. (1971), 'Ideology and Ideological State Apparatuses', in *Lenin and
    Philosophy and Other Essays*, New Left Books, London, pp.127–186
Annove, R. F. et al (1996), 'A Political Sociology of Education and Development in
    Latin America', *International Journal of Comparative Sociology*, vol.XXXVII,
    nos1–2, June, pp. 140–158

Barker, R. (1990), *Political Legitimacy and the State*, Clarendon, Oxford
Barry, A. (1994), 'Harmonization and the art of European government', in C. Roots
    and H. Davis (eds), *A New Europe? Social Change and Political Transformation*,
    UCL Press, London, pp. 39–54
Becker, G. S. (1975), *Human Capital: A Theoretical and Empirical Analysis, with
    Special Reference to Education*, National Bureau of Economic Research, New
    York
Beetham, D. (1991), *The Legitimation of Power*, Macmillan, Basingstoke
Beukel, E. (1994), 'Reconstructing Integration Theory: The Case of Education Policy
    in the EC', *Cooperation and Conflict*, vol.29, no.1, pp.33–54
Blaug, M. (1992a), 'The Empirical Status of Human Capital Theory', in his (ed),
    The Economic Value of Education: Studies in the Economics of Education,
    Edward Elgar Publishing, Aldershot (Hants), pp.1–31
Blaug, M. (1992b), 'Where Are We Now in the Economics of Education?', in his (ed),
    The Economic Value of Education: Studies in the Economics of Education,
    Edward Elgar Publishing, Aldershot (Hants), pp. 211–22
Bowels, S. and Gintis, H. (1975), 'The Problem With Human Capital Theory –
    A Marxian Critique', *American Economic Review*, vol.65, no.2, May, pp.74–82
Bowels, S. and Gintis, H. (1976), *Schooling in Capitalist America*, Routledge & Kegan
    Paul, London
Boyd, W. (1911), *The Educational Theory of Jean Jacques Rousseau*, Longmans,
    London
Bray, M. (1990), 'The Economics of Education', in R. Murray Thomas (ed),
    International Comparative Education: Practices, Issues and Prospects, Pergamon
    Press, Oxford, pp.253–273
Brock, C. and Tulasiewicz, W.(eds) (1994), *Education in a Single Europe*, Routledge,
    London, especially the Introduction
Burston, W. H. (1973), *James Mill Philosophy and Education*, The Alhlone Press,
    London
Byre, A. (1992), *EC Social Policy and 1992: Laws, cases and materials*, Kluwer Law
    and Taxation Publishers, Boston (see ch.9 on Vocational Training)

Carnoy, M. (1992), 'Education and Economic Development', in M. Blaug (ed) *The Economic Value of Education: Studies in the Economics of Education*, Edward Elgar Publishing, Aldershot (Hants), pp.339–359

Cheallaigh, M. N. (1995), *Apprenticeship in the EU Member States*, Cedefop, Office for Official Publications of the European Communities, Brussels

Chisholm, L. (1992), 'A crazy quilt: education, training and social change in Europe', in J. Bailey (ed), *Social Europe*, Longman, London, pp.123–146

Collins, H. (1993), *European Vocational Education Systems*, Kogan Page, London

Coulby, D. and Jones, C. (1995), *Postmodernity and European Education Systems*, Trentham Books, London

Cremona, M. (1995), 'Citizens of third countries: movement and employment of migrant workers within the European Union', *Legal Issues of European Integration*, no.2, pp.87–113

Cullen, H. (1996), 'From Migrants to Citizens? European Community Policy on International Education', *International and Comparative Law Quarterly*, vol.45, no.1, January, pp.109–129

Dale, R. (ed) (1985), *Education, Training and Employment: Towards a New Vocationalism*, Pergamon Press, Oxford

Dalichow, F. (1987), 'Academic Recognition within the European Community', *European Journal of Education*, vol.22, no.1, pp.39–58

Dashwood, A. (1981), 'The Harmonisation Process', in C. C. Twitchett (ed), *Harmonisation in the EEC*, Macmillan Press, London, pp.7–17

Delors, J. et al (1996), *Learning: The Treasure Within*, Report to UNESCO of the International Commission on Education for the Twenty-first Century, UNESCO Publishing, Paris

Donald, J. (1992), 'Dewey-eyed Optimism: The Possibility of Democratic Education', *New Left Review*, no.192, March/April, pp.133–144.

Emiliou, N. (1992), 'Subsidiarity: An Effective Barrier Against "the Enterprises of Ambition"', *European Law Review*, vol.17, pp.383–407

Entwistle, H. (1979), *Antonio Gramsci: Conservative Schooling for Radical Politics*, Routledge & Kegan Paul, London

Fogg, K. and Jones, H. (1985), 'Educating the European Community: Ten Years On', *European Journal of Education*, vol.20, nos.2–3, pp.293–300

Freedland, M. (1996), 'Vocational Training in EC Law and Policy: Education, Employment or Welfare?', *Industrial Law Review*, vol.25, no.2, June, pp.110–120

Friedl, B. (1996), 'Fixed term contracts for foreign language lecturers: A proportionate restriction on free movement of workers?', *Industrial Law Journal*, vol.25, no.2, March, pp.66–70

Funnell, P. and Muller, D. (eds) (1991), *Vocational Education and the Challenge of Europe*, Kogan Page, London

Garcia, S. (ed.) (1993), *European Identity and the Search for Legitimacy*, Pinter, London

Garforth, F. W. (1979), *John Stuart Mill's Theory of Education*, Martin Robertson, Oxford

Golub, J. (1996), 'Sovereignty and Subsidiarity in the EC Environmental Policy', *Political Studies*, vol.XLIV, pp.686–703

Hagen, J. (1987), 'University Cooperation and Academic Recognition in Europe: the Council of Europe and the Communities', *European Journal of Education*, vol.22, no.1, pp.77–83

Hantrais, L. (1995), *Social Policy in the European Union*, Macmillan Press, London, especially chs2–3

Harrison, V.(1996), 'Subsidiarity in Article 3b of the EC Treaty: Gobbledegook or Justiciable Principle?', *International and Comparative Law Quarterly*, vol.45, no.2, April, pp.431–439

Holmes, B. (1992), 'The Common Origins of and Modern Differences between European Systems of European Education: A Comparative Perspective', in M. Whitehead (ed) *Education and Europe: Historical and Contemporary Perspectives*, The University of Hull, Hull, pp.128–147

Hopkins, K. et al (1994), *Into the Heart of Europe: The Education Dimension*, National Foundation for Educational Research, Slough (Berks)

Hussain, A. (1976), 'The economy and the educational system in capitalist societies', *Economy and Society*, vol.5, no.4, November, pp.413–434

IRDAC (Industrial Research and Development Advisory Committee of the European Commission) (1994), *Quality and Relevance: The Challenge to European Education: Unlocking Europe's Human Potential*, Brussels

Jarvis, M. (1996), 'Freedom of establishment and freedom to provide services: Lawyers on the move?', *European Law Review*, vol.21, no.3, June, pp.247–252

Johnes, G. (1993), *The Economics of Education*, The Macmillan Press, London

Kokulsing, K., Ainley, P. and Tysome, T. (1996), *Beyond Competence: The National Council for Vocational Qualifications Framework and the Challenge to Higher Education in the New Millenium*, Avebury, Aldershot

Kühnhardt, L. (1992), 'Federalism and Subsidiarity', *Telos*, no.91, March, pp.77–86

Laslett, J. M. (1990), 'The Mutual Recognition of Diplomas, Certificates and other Evidence of Formal Qualifications in the European Community', *Legal Issues of European Integration*, no.1, pp.1–53

Lenaerts, K. (1994), 'Education in the European Community Law after 'Maastricht', *'Common Market Law Review*, vol.31, pp.7–41

Lenzen, D. (1996), 'Education and Training in Europe?', in D. Benner and D. Lenzen (eds), *Education for the New Europe*, Berghahn Books, Oxford, pp.7–28

Lonbay, J. (1989), 'Education and Law: The Community Context', *European Law Review*, December, pp.363–387

Lowe, J. (1992), 'Education and European Integration', *International Review of Education*, vol.38, no.6, pp.579–590

Mallinson, V. (1980), *The Western European Idea in Education*, Pergamon Press, Oxford

Marquand, D. (1994), 'Reinventing Federalism: Europe and the Left', *New Left Review*, no.203, January/February, pp.17–26

Marshall, A. (1920[1890]), *Principles of Economics*, Macmillan Press, London

Marx, K. (1977[1846]), 'The German Ideology', in *Selected Writings*, edited by D. McLellan, Oxford University Press, Oxford, pp.159–191

Mckeen, W. (1994), 'The Radical Potential of the European Community's Equality Legislation', *Studies in Political Economy*, no.43, Spring, pp.117–136

McMahon, J. A. (1995), *Education and Culture in European Community Law*, The
    Athlone Press, London
Miliband, R. (1974), *The State in Capitalist Society*, Quarter Books, London
Mill, J. (1992[1823]), *Political Writings*, edited by T. Ball, Cambridge University
    Press, Cambridge, especially the essay on education
Mill, J. S. (1991[1859]), *On Liberty and Other Essays*, edited by John Gray, Oxford
    University Press, Oxford
Mill, J. S. (1878), *Principles of Political Economy*, in two volumes, Longmans,
    London
Mincer, J. (1992), 'Human Capital and Labor Market', in M. Blaug (ed) *The
    Economic Value of Education*, Edward Elgar Publishing, Aldershot (Hants),
    pp.186–193
Mitch, D. (1992), 'Education and Economic Growth', in M. Blaug (ed), *The Economic
    Value of Education*, Edward Elgar Publishing, Aldershot (Hants), pp.385–401
Moschonas, A. (1996), 'The Logic of European Integration', in G. Kourvetaris and
    A. Moschonas (eds), *The Impact of European Integration: Political, Sociological
    and Economic Changes*, Praeger, Westport, pp.9–38
Mulcahy, D. G. (1991), 'In Search of the European Dimension in Education',
    European Journal of Teacher Education, vol.14, no.3, pp.213–226
Munch, J. (1995), *Vocational Education and Training in the Federal Republic of
    Germany*, Cedefop, Office for Official Publications of the European
    Communities, Brussels

Neave, G. (1984), *The EEC and Education*, Trentham Books, European Institute of
    Education and Social Policy, Trentham
Neave, G. (1985), 'The Non-State Sector in Education in Europe: a conceptual and
    historical analysis', *European Journal of Education*, vol.20, no.4, pp.321–337
Nielsen, S. P. (1995), *Vocational Education and Training in Denmark*, Cedefop, Office
    for Official Publications of the European Communities, Brussels

O'Connor, J. (1973), *The Fiscal Crisis of the State*, St. Martin's Press, New York
OECD (1992), *High-Quality Education and Training for All*, OECD, Paris
O' Neill, M. (1996), *The Politics of European Integration*, Routledge, London and
    New York

Papadopoulos, G. S. (1994), *Education, 1960–1990: The OECD Perspective*, OECD,
    Paris
Pelkmans, J. (1987), 'The new approach to technical harmonisation and
    standardisation', *Journal of Common Market Studies*, vol.25, no.3, March,
    pp.249–269
Pierson, P. (1996), 'The Path to European Integration: A Historical Institutionalist
    Analysis', *Comparative Political Studies*, vol.29, no.2, April, pp.123–163
Poulantzas, N. (1975), *Political Power and Social Classes*, NLB, London
Pryce, R. (1973), *The Politics of the European Community*, Butterworths, London

Ringer, F. K. (1979), *Education and Society in Modern Europe*, Indiana University
    Press, Bloomington and London, [see especially the 'Introduction: Concepts and
    Hypotheses' (pp.1–31)]
Roots, C. A. (1996), 'Political Sociology in Britain: Survey of the Literature and the
    Profession', *Current Sociology*, vol.44, no.3, Winter, pp.108–131

Rosenthal, G. G. (1991), 'Education and Training Policy', in L. Hurwitz and C. Lequesne (eds), *The State of the European Community*, Lynne Reinner Publishers, Longman, pp.273–283

Ross, M. (1989), 'Mutual Recognition of Professional Qualifications', *European Law Review*, vol.14, pp.162–166

Rousseau, J.-J. (1966[1762]), *The Social Contract and Discourses*, translated by G. D. H. Cole, Everyman's Library, London

Rousseau, J.-J. (1979[1762]), *Emile (on Education)*, introduction and translation by Allan Bloom, Basic Books, New York

Schofield, H. (1972), *The Philosophy of Education*, George Allen and Unwin, London

Schultz, T. W. (1961), 'Investment in Human Capital', *American Economic Review*, vol.51, no.1, March, pp.1–17

Scott, A. et al (1994), 'Subsidiarity: A 'Europe of the Regions' vs. the British Constitution?', *Journal of Common Market Studies*, vol.32, no.1 March, pp.47– 67

Slot, P. J. (1996), 'Harmonisation', *European Law Review*, vol.21, no.5, pp.378–397

Smith, A. (1961[1776]), *The Wealth of Nations*, Methuen, London

Smith, A. (1985), 'Higher Education Cooperation 1975–1985: creating a basis for growth in an adverse economic climate', *European Journal of Education*, vol.20, nos2–3, pp.267–292

Soskice, D. W. (1993), 'Social Skills from Mass Higher Education: Rethinking the Company-Based Initial Training Paradigm', *Oxford Review of Economic Policy*, vol.9, no.3, pp.101–113

Sprokkereef, A. (1995), 'Developments in European Community education policy', in J. Lodge (ed), *The European Community and the Challenge of the Future*, 2nd edition, Pinter Publishers, London

Stavrou, S. (1995), *Vocational Education and Training in Greece*, Cedefop, Office for Official Publications of the European Communities, Brussels

Stubb, A. C.-G. 'A Categorization of Differentiated Integration', *Journal of Common Market Studies*, vol.34, no.2, June, pp.283–295

Taylor, P. (1996), *The European Union in the 1990s*, Oxford University Press, Oxford

Teasdale, A.L. (1993), 'Subsidiarity in Post-Maastricht Europe', *Political Quarterly*, vol.64, no.2, pp.187–197

Thurow, L. C. (1970), *Investment in Human Capital*, Wadsworth Publishing, Belmon (Cal.)

Torres, C. A, 'State and Education: Marxist Theories', in T. Husen and T. N. Postlethwaite (eds), *The International Encyclopedia of Education*, Pergamon Press, Oxford, pp.4793–4798

Toth, A. G. (1992), 'The Principle of Subsidiarity in the Maastricht Treaty', *Common Market Law Review*, vol.29, no.6, 1079–1105

Touraine, A. (1994), 'European countries in a post-national era', in C. Rootes and H. Davis (eds.), *Social Change and Political Transformation*, UCL Press, pp.13–26

USA (American Report of the National Commission on Excellence in Education), (1983). *A Nation at Risk: The Imperative for Educational Reform*, US Congress, Washington DC

Vaizey, J. (1962),*The Economics of Education,* Faber and Faber, London

Van Kersbergen, K. and Verbeek, B. (1994), 'The politics of Subsidiarity in the European Union', *Journal of Common Market Studies,* vol.32, no.2, June, pp.215–236

Vignes, D. (1990), 'The Harmonisation of National Legislation and the EEC', *European Law Review,* vol.15, October, pp.358–374

Waegenbaur, R. (1986), 'Free Movement in the Professions: The New EEC Proposal on Professional Qualifications', *Common Market Law Review,* vol.23, pp.91–109

Watson, P. (1987), 'Court of Justice Cases: A Comment on Gravier', *Common Market Law Review,* vol.24, pp.89–97

Watson, P. (1992), 'Wandering Students: Their Rights under Community Law', in D. Curtin and D. O'Keeffe (eds), *Constitutional Adjudication in European Community and National Law,* Butterworth, Dublin, pp.79–88

West, E. G. (1992), 'The Role of Education in Nineteenth-Century Doctrines of Political Economy', in M. Blaug (ed), *The Economic Value of Education: Studies in the Economics of Education,* Edward Elgar Publishing, Aldershot (Hants), pp.493–504

White, R. (1995), 'Children and Rights to Education under Article 12 of Regulation 1612/68', *European Law Review,* vol.2, no.5, October, pp.501–507

Willems, J.-P. (1995),*Vocational Education and Training in France,* Cedefop, Office for Publications of the European Communities, Brussels

Index

157